A Celebration of Bees

A
Celebration
of Bees

Helping Children
Write Poetry

Barbara Juster Esbensen

Foreword by Lee Bennett Hopkins

HENRY HOLT AND COMPANY
NEW YORK

Henry Holt and Company, Inc.
Publishers since 1866
115 West 18th Street
New York, New York 10011

Henry Holt® is a registered
trademark of Henry Holt and Company, Inc.

LIBRARY OF CONGRESS CATALOGING-IN-PUBLICATION DATA
Esbensen, Barbara Juster.
A celebration of bees: helping children write poetry /
Barbara Juster Esbensen.
    p.   cm.
Includes bibliographical references.
1. Poetry—Study and teaching.   2. Children as authors.
I. Title.
PN1101.E8   199595-18516
808.   1—dc20CIP

ISBN 0-8050-3764-0
ISBN 0-8050-3765-9 (An Owl Book: pbk.)

Henry Holt books are available for special promotions and premiums.
For details contact: Director, Special Markets.

First published in 1975 by Winston Press, Inc.

First Edition—1995

Designed by Kathryn Parise

Printed in the United States of America
All first editions are printed on acid-free paper. ∞

1   3   5   7   9   10   8   6   4   2
1   3   5   7   9   10   8   6   4   2 (pbk.)

Grateful acknowledgment is made for permission
to reprint the following: Haiku by Bashō from *An Introduction to
Haiku* by Harold G. Henderson; Copyright © 1968 by Harold G. Henderson;
Used by Permission of Doubleday, a division of Bantam Doubleday Dell
Publishing Group, Inc. "Triad" from *Verse* by Adelaide Crapsey; Copyright ©
1922 by Algernon S. Crapsey and renewed 1950 by The Adelaide Crapsey
Foundation; Reprinted by permission of Alfred A. Knopf, Inc. "South-
bound roaring past . . ." by Anne Rutherford from *Borrowed Water:
A Book of American Haiku* by the Los Altos Writers Roundtable;
Copyright © 1966; Reprinted by permission of
Charles E. Tuttle Co., Inc. of Tokyo, Japan.

For my son
Peter Neil Esbensen
1951–1970
His dust is brighter
than all the air.

Contents

Acknowledgments

Over the years, I have collected many of the poems written for me in widely scattered classrooms all over the country. The young poets are grown up now, but their work remains as the fresh expressions they created when they pushed their imaginations as far as they could go. My thanks to them.

My own children, Julie, Peter, Daniel, Jane, George, and Kai, have allowed me to include their poems, so I thank them all. I want to speak especially of Peter, whose interest in my creative work with children was unflagging and enthusiastic. This is the book he hoped I'd write. He died before he could see it and find his poem printed in these pages.

I owe a debt of gratitude to Lee Bennett Hopkins and Jeffrey Copeland. They felt so strongly that *A Celebration of Bees*, first published in 1975, should be back in print, that their enthusiasm was catching! This new edition is the result. Lee has generously written the foreword, and Jeff provided the excellent, up-to-the-minute bibliography.

My thanks to Donald Hurst. Long ago he said these magic words: "I'd like you to write down how you get kids to think poetry."

Foreword

How exciting it is to have *A Celebration of Bees* back in print. Over the past two decades since the volume first appeared, numerous journal articles and professional textbooks have been published discussing varied writing theories. Few, however, contain the down-to-earth, hands-on, tried-and-tested approach offered here by Barbara Juster Esbensen, an accomplished poet and recipient of the 1994 National Council of Teachers of English Award for Excellence in Children's Poetry for her aggregate body of work.

Those who have had the privilege of listening to Esbensen's stimulating presentations know the contagious enthusiasm she exudes regarding children and their creation of poetry. *A Celebration of Bees* is the next best thing to take you into her world, to stir your senses, to bring marvelous magic into homes and classrooms, to unleash and spark children to write.

Touching on universal subjects, from the seasons to city life, from animals to the inanimate, Esbensen has the power to shake us up and cause us to see the potential inherent in all children. We witness the development of young writers, from those beginning to experiment with words, language and verse forms, to the more sophisticated students. We watch them attain the skills necessary to hone, polish, and think through their poetic compositions with the sensitive guidance of this first-rate teacher and poet.

You *will* celebrate this sound, refreshing approach to releasing inner talents of students, and you *will* celebrate the results of children's achievements. Most important, children themselves will come to realize that learning to appreciate poetry and the craft of writing it is a satisfying and integral part of their lives.

Lee Bennett Hopkins
Scarborough, New York

Poetry is a dream
breathing
its way out of my mind.
It runs to places
where colors
   are p-o-u-r- i-n-g
the words
into the beating head.

— Tina, age 10

Author's Note

When I was in high school, my creative writing teacher Eulalie C. Beffel (1905–1994) did the kinds of things to motivate her fifteen young writers that I later tried to do with my students.

Without her imaginative teaching, I would not have been able to write this book. She once wrote, quoting an early poem of mine, that she hoped my students would:

> split the shining ruby
> and find the star inside!

That is what this book is all about.

Barbara Juster Esbensen
Edina, Minnesota
1995

A
Celebration
of Bees

There is nobody
that can explain
Summer
except the eye.

The smell of hot
sweat.
The forest fires
blazing and crackling,
the bees orange
and black fur.

The bees. I'll
never forget
the BUZZ!
        BUZZ!

Introduction

"Is *swagger* a word? It is, ain't it, teacher?"
This is Susan. Her untidy red hair needs a
barrette. As usual, tiny, mean points of light
blaze in her defiant pale green eyes. Susan
is ten, and she hates school. She hates the
third grade with double intensity because
she hated it last year, too. Susan hates reading books. She has not learned how to read
well, and all books seem to exist just to trip

her up. Her reading vocabulary on achievement tests is somewhere around first grade.

But she is asking about a word. A fine word: *swagger.*

"Yes," I tell her, "*swagger* is a word." Does she know what it
means?

"Yeah, I know," she answers with a wild flipping of that lank,
red skein. On her way back to her seat, down the long aisle of old
desks bolted to the floor, Susan stops. She gives a boy one tri-
umphant, hard whack on the head with the flat of her hand.

"Ha," she crows, "swagger *is too* a word and here it goes, right
in my old poem!"

And then, with a final glower she adds, to the other thirty-four
children, "and don't *nobody* else use it neither!" She flounces off
to her seat. Nobody else uses it.

Later, when Susan, the nonreading, belligerent, school-hating
Susan, stands before the class to read her poem, this is what we
hear:

RAIN
Rain swaggers across the street
Rain skips across the alleys
        of the world . . .

In the third grade that year, thirty-five children from a "culturally deprived" neighborhood in a northern California city wrote
their heads off. They wrote about everything and anything, as fast
as ideas and images formed, with no concern about exact punctuation and perfect spelling. That would come later, with the polishing, with the writing of the thing beautifully on the coveted
sixth grade paper, very white with no holes and with bright blue
lines. Their excitement, pride, and enthusiasm about writing
carried into other subjects as well, perhaps because of the

general atmosphere of successful personal achievement one could feel in the classroom. Writing became, for each of the children, a means to explore language, self, attitudes, and one's awareness of the world of real and imaginary things.

"Night," another nonreader told us in his poem, "is a black panther waiting to strike." Margie's parents had wanted to keep her in grade two another year because she seemed quite baffled by the printed word, and yet Margie could write an evocation of falling asleep, "the beds move in the night. . . ."

This book will set out for you the techniques I have found to be effective in generating enthusiastic responses to words and their creative uses. What I am trying to find with children and young people and what they and you, their parents and teachers, must constantly look for are new ways to make our language express familiar experiences. We are looking for expression that is fresh, new, uniquely the writer's own.

A friend of mine, one hot, humid day in St. Paul, asked her two daughters to think of words that would describe the incredible heat. My friend, who is a writer, wanted her children to search their vocabularies for strong "heat words." They did some delighted brainstorming and thought of words like *boiling* and *melt* and *steam* and *sweat*. They came up with *scorch* and *fry*, and when their mother asked, "What other things can be hot?" one of the children shouted, "Red pepper!"

They thought of some words that were the opposite of "hot" too. Their mother told them that opposite ideas and images can often give strength to one another.

(Think about it. What "cold" words can you think of, just off the top of your head?) As the words came to mind, the children and their mother said them aloud, and all three wrote them on sheets of paper until the paper was covered.

Nine-year-old Jessica wrote this poem that summer day:

My mother is calling but
I can't find her
in the steam.
I am starting to melt
like butter frying in a pan
sizzling
to a sweaty smell.
And the light is like boiling water
vaporing up.

Is the neighbor's house burning?
Chimney tumbling like a slow waterfall
into bubbling yellow grass?
Roof shouts out fireworks.
It puts red pepper in my mouth
and makes my eyes water
with heat and hate
and love.

Something reaches out to grab me.
It's my mother's ice cool hands.
Safe.

—JESSICA

One evening, shortly after I had received a Siamese kitten, my
children and I sat down and wrote "kitten words." We were especially delighted with this kitty, because he had six toes on one of
his feet! We watched the lively little cat ricochet around the living
room, and my daughter Julie, who was fifteen at the time, wrote:

The small dark half-face of
the Siamese kitten dashes about
the house,

hiding under the waves of
cushions on the sofa—
stalking unsuspecting feet
from the dark safety under chairs.

On paws soft as old dandelions,
the kitten crouches, leaps, and
stuns.
Hunter!

Blurs, shades of browns
stop.
The "kill" is over.
The dark half-face reflects
with kitten innocence—

and washes its twenty-one toes!

—JULIE

Poetry as we use it here means language that excites. It means finding and using those surprising and just-right combinations of words that will delight us and astonish us with their newness.

Perhaps we forget something about our English language, since it is so commonplace a thing to us who speak it from birth. But it is interesting to know that English has been described by linguists to be one of the richest in the world. The writer Joseph Conrad was Polish. He spoke French, then learned English as an officer on English merchant ships. And when he began to write his great books, he said he never for an instant hesitated about the language he would use for his novels. He chose English for its tremendous variety, its shades of meaning, its richness, and its color.

It is this richness and variety that excites children and encourages them to play with words, to enjoy words for their sound, their color, and even for the shape of a particular word on the page.

As we look at what schoolchildren sometimes write as "poems," we can see that many teachers don't really know what real quality their students are capable of producing and that they have had no experience with ways to start young minds percolating with ideas. In these pages you will find hundreds of examples of poetry by children of all ages. And you will be able to see what sorts of questions one can ask young writers to consider, what kinds of probing and yet more probing must be pushed by the teacher or by a parent before anything of value happens in the mind.

One June day when one of our children, George, was five years old, he rushed inside from the garden. Breathless, he dashed upstairs to find me.

"Mom!" he yelled. "Come quick! There's a celebration of bees out there."

Now *that's* poetry!

Later, when he was in second grade, he came home with a whole page of "poems" written by the class members.

"She says all the poems have to rhyme," he told me. And I read his "poem":

A warm day
Is a May day
I lay in the hay
And hope to stay.

The rest of the efforts on the page—all titled "A Warm Day"—were nearly identical to his dismal collection of boring words. There was no attempt, obviously, to get those children to explore the idea of a warm day with their senses, with their lively children's minds, with enthusiasm. It's a far cry indeed from that jubilant "celebration of bees" shouted by a preschooler to the dull emptiness of day-hay-stay "poems" written for the second grade teacher.

An emphasis on strong verbs and lively, unexpected adjectives carries over into disciplines other than the language arts, of course. Social studies or science reports, for instance, will come to life if the student has had ongoing experience using language in effective ways. The whole language approach, used in many schools, encourages a cross-disciplinary emphasis on writing and reading.

When people write creatively, they are actually seeing familiar objects or sensations or situations as though for the very first time. George said "a celebration of bees" because his uninhibited fresh mind felt that a swarm of bees, the sunlit garden, the sounds of early summer bird songs were a festive, lively, *celebration:* an accurate image. At three, Kai, another of our sons, excitedly told his father that the noisy fire in the big cabin fireplace was "roaring like a tiger" and that it was "waving like a flag." The huge blaze impressed him. He wanted to speak about it, so he compared it with two other things that immediately occurred to him. It is this spontaneous delight in words and self-expression that the techniques I've used throughout this book will help to encourage. I have found these techniques to be just about 100 percent effective, whether I've used them with seven- or eight-year-olds, junior high school students, college people, or adults. They work equally well with people I meet regularly as a writing class and with children I've never seen before, and they work just as well at home as in the classroom.

The poems you will read here were written by all sorts of children from every kind of background and degree of cultural stimulation. There are poems here by children from comfortable loving families, and by boys and girls from broken homes, from squalid surroundings and bitter parents. These children live in cities whose populations range from 30,000 to nearly 500,000 and represent both seacoasts, the South, and the northern Midwest. The poems from Micronesia were written by young people, some of whom had never seen a city at all.

In an accepting environment, the magic of the written word becomes for all of them a means to add something to their lives and to soar above the commonplace, the trite, the used.

Wordplay can be an activity for you and your children anytime, any place. On a car trip with your children, for example, you can focus on color words to describe the sky, perhaps, or something in the landscape. Have pads of paper and pencils close at hand, kept in the car for just this purpose, so that all the words can be set down as they are dreamed up. Maybe a blank book for each child would be a great idea. These word lists can grow richer and more motivating as the words occur to you and your young traveler. Push your child to compare the sky's color to something else, for example: What bird has this color on its feathers? What insect is this color? Is a storm approaching? Compare the darkening clouds with something else. What do the cloud shapes remind us of?

What is the texture of the road or the ground or the hillsides? What else looks like this—an animal? a person? Look at the trees against the sky. How do those branches feel against the sky? If your hands were twigs, how would they touch the sky?

What word describes the sound of a truck passing the car? What can we compare this truck to as it passes us?

You can see that this sort of game can go on and on. There is no limit to the possibilities, of course. If you start thinking this way, your children will no doubt surpass you in coming up with off-the-wall ideas! The important thing to realize is that the possibilities of using our everyday language to create unexpected images are endless.

The book will show you one way of releasing the creative impulse that we all possess. Perhaps you have your own way of getting your children interested in writing. There must be as many ways as there are people who love children's writing. There may be, even so, one or two ideas here that you can add to your own. If you have never tried to encourage children to write creatively, I hope this book will give you a way to begin.

What's in a Word

Emily Dickinson wrote in a letter once that if she should read something that made her feel "so cold no fire can warm me," and if the words made her feel as though "the top of my head were blown off," then she knew she was reading poetry.

When talking about poetry with children, I emphasize again and again that the poet wants to use our ordinary, everyday language in new ways; to make that language open new doors and windows for us; and to let us see old familiar things as though we'd never seen them before.

Experimenting with the idea of wishing on a star, and wanting to say it in a new way, this is what sixth grader Angie wrote:

The shimmering sky
holds every twinkling star.
Every twinkling star
holds an avalanche of wishes.

Two elements of good writing are evident here: Those strong words, *shimmering*, *twinkling*, and *avalanche*, make us sit up and take notice! The repetition of "every twinkling star" gives a nice sense of rhythm to the whole poem.

When eleven-year-old Melissa wanted to think of words that

"felt gray" to her, she came up with some interesting images. When you read this poem, you can tell exactly what words occurred to her as a starting point:

Gray,
a shiver of color
standing alone
with no one to hold it.
Gray,
cold—frozen in time.
Gray,
color of old things,
brushing
its lonely color
everywhere.

Any good descriptive writing can be "poetry" in this sense. Indeed, the book *A Stone, A Leaf, A Door* (Charles Scribner's Sons, 1948), edited by John S. Barnes, is the prose of Thomas Wolfe, culled from all of thousands of pages of his novels, set out on the page in short lines, and made brief enough so the impact of the words can hit us.

Writing poetry encourages children to be accurate, to say what they really mean, and to say it as economically as possible. No special language is necessary. No stylistic trimmings or tricks are necessary. What *is* necessary is to seek and find words that can capture the feelings and impressions we call experience, the all but inaudible music we sense in ourselves. To do this, we need not go down the June-moon-spittoon-baboon trail searching frantically for rhyming words. Poetry does not have to rhyme, or look a certain way on the page, or have lines that have a certain basic rhythm pattern. Today poetry is a capturing of essences, and words are the traps we set to do the job. Anything is fair game for the poet. There are no right subjects—and no wrong ones either. The books of poetry in the bibliography at the end of the book will show you how diverse this world of poetry is for the contemporary reader.

In the pages to follow, you will meet the poems of Elvira M., a California third grader. When she came to my classroom, she was Spanish-speaking, with an incredible facility for the English language. For a solid year, Elvira wrote poems full of delicious images, like this one from our "Rain" section:

> When the raindrops fall
> on a puddle,
> They look like shooting-stars
> in the blue mud-puddle sky.

In her "Wind" poem, she says the wind ". . . blows my hair / like purple thistles / in the sky. . . ."

When Elvira went into the fourth grade, we moved back to the Midwest, and she wrote to me fairly regularly for several years sending me her latest poems, which had undergone a sad change. One, written in fourth grade and called "The Butterfly," had these lines in it:

> The butterfly that went by
> To me once she said hi.

And the last weary verse went:

> Right now she's in heaven,
> with 007.
> Where she will flitter and flutter
> With her wings as yellow as butter.

"Did you like them?" she asks at the end of her three-page letter full of similar work. "I think they're sort of . . . well I don't know. But I don't like them too much. Mrs. N. tells us poems have to rhyme."

From sixth grade, I received a letter from Elvira bearing the same edict: "I have not written any poems . . . because at my room Mrs. C. makes us write poems that rhyme and I cannot seem to make any that rhyme." Then she includes one "That I just wrote anyway. Not for Mrs. C.":

> The yellow and orange
> flowers
> are glittering
> in the sun.
> They want to go
> to London,
> to Paris,
> and
> New York.

I hope this has convinced you *never* to say "a poem *has* to rhyme." Generally speaking, I ask children not to use rhyme. It slows up the torrent of shapes, tastes, sounds, and colors that want to find places on their papers. Children will spend time lurching down the alphabet to find the rhyming words—and you'll end up with meaningless poems instead of the kinds of things children do best. Occasionally a poem "feels like rhyming." A few are included here, and those few somehow avoid the deadly singsong characteristic of rhymes done by children.

I've lost track of Elvira over the years. One of the last letters I received from her when she was in the seventh grade asked me if I had saved "the poems I wrote when I was in third grade." She asked me to send them to her. She was recalling some isolated single lines from memory and, obviously, contrasting them with the awful doggerel she was currently writing. I sent her poems to her, and I hope she still has them, for they have the unmistakable ring and flow of real poetry. When she was only a child, she was a creative writer. The stifling of that free-flying attitude toward words is unforgivable.

My hope is that this book will help you discover other Elviras among the children you know. Perhaps there are some waiting in your home, pencils poised, ready to write!

Some Ways to Use This Book

Each of the chapters deals with a particular subject you might want to use in introducing poetry writing to children. They can be used in any order at all, except that I suggest you expose your young writers to cinquains before they tackle haiku, and those two chapters are arranged that way.

To get an overview of all the possibilities the book offers, you might want to read it straight through. On the other hand, if circumstances push you toward a particular subject or topic, start there.

The children's poems I have included can be helpful when you want to let your young writers hear what others who are their age have written. If you are new to this whole area of poetry writing by children and young people, these poems can afford you some insight into the capabilities of writers of a variety of ages.

At the end of the book are listed books of poetry whose quality and intent will show you and your children the diversity and beauty of contemporary (and almost contemporary) poetry. Some of these books are anthologies. Others are by a single poet.

It is essential that children's work be reproduced from time to time for everyone to read. Just typing one example, at least, from *each* young writer and making copies for everyone will give the new poets the satisfaction of seeing their work in print with a byline. Occasionally, I've had a student who wanted to remain anonymous or who used initials only, or a pen name. Fair enough.

A collection of each child's poems can be stapled together, with illustrations and a cover. This "publishing" gives prestige to the child's creations and validity to the whole idea that good writing has a right to be preserved and read over and over. In some schools, the finished booklets are placed in the library for a time so that children can read one another's work.

At home, too, you can honor your child's work by placing it in a bookshelf, along with other books. The important thing is the respect given to a child's creative efforts.

Although spelling and punctuation are not our concern when we're in the white heat of writing images and ideas on paper, it is important to attend to some of the mechanics of writing when the poem is formed at last. I like to ask students to give me a copy of their work and to keep a dated copy for themselves.

This "finished copy" is the one the writers have checked to make sure words are spelled correctly and sentences are punctuated so they make sense to the reader. I emphasize that because the poem is now a completed fact, a creation, it deserves to be presented so it can be easily understood and appreciated.

It is from my collection of finished copy that I can select poems for reproducing. Sometimes with older students, my collection is turned over to a group of student editors who do the selecting, always making certain that each student is represented by at least one piece. If you have done a good job of pushing young minds to think of "a better word, now a better one than that—now a stronger one than those two," there will be, in each child's work, something worthy of reprinting.

Enthusiasm for writing, a dawning realization that words are power, and a comfortable feeling about the whole business will pay off in many ways. We spoke of Susan at the beginning of this introduction. When Susan's poetry was printed, along with pieces by the other third graders, it turned out that Susan and the other nonreaders could, indeed, read after all. They could read their own work and things written by the others. Slowly they began to get the idea about words. They began to have the glimmer of a feeling that words in books are after all just words "any old person" can put down for someone to read. Their active distrust of the snaky sentences and shifty punctuation on the printed pages of their books began to give way to this new understanding. Writing and reading are irrevocably linked.

And Now, Before I Say Anything

A college professor used to say, "Now, before I say anything this morning, I want to say something." Before I begin to talk about techniques that will help children to write, I, too, "want to say something."

If any one word can stand for the essence of creating a climate, an atmosphere that allows the creative impulse to grow and flourish, I think it would be the word *accepting*. Every child needs to feel that you respect and accept what he or she is trying to do. This does not imply dishonest praise for something that is not as good as it can be. It means that you exhibit an underlying understanding and respect for the children's efforts, while trying to bring out of those children the most exciting ideas they are capable of having.

It means that you can look for and find in their work something of real or potential value, something that can be talked about seriously with a view toward strengthening it, if necessary, toward making it the child's own best effort.

Let me give you an example of some give-and-take between child and teacher.

BJE: Who has a good strong word to show how a cat moves?

TIM: I wrote, "The cat moves slowly."

BJE: I can certainly see that cat as he goes so slowly along, Tim. I wonder if you could paint us a *clearer* word picture of what you are seeing in your mind. Let's see if there is a single word that means "move slowly," the way you want us to see your cat moving.

TIM: How about *creeps*? The cat is moving slowly because it is after a bird. *Creeps* shows that, doesn't it?

BJE: *Creeps* is a good word. Can you tell me why it is even better than "moves slowly"?

TIM: Because the word *creeps* lets you see the cat slung down along the ground after the bird. "Moves slowly" didn't show us how he looked at all.

BJE: Perhaps we can list even more words that are like *creeps*. Let's put them on the board for other children to use. . . .

Every step of the way I've tried to show acceptance, respect, and understanding for this child, even while he is encouraged to *improve* the quality of his self-expression. Nowhere do I say, "That's a dull way to write," or "You can certainly do better than *that*, Tim."

In a truly relaxed atmosphere, where only constructive criticism is offered by the children and by the parent or teacher, any child will be able to develop real powers of written expression. There is, in this kind of learning environment, no fear of ridicule, no agony of embarrassment, no sullen responses to repeated failure. No child will be unwilling to risk some far-out images, some grand experiments with the sound, color, texture, shape, or taste of language.

Can you maintain this climate? You must, or your efforts are doomed to fail. As a matter of fact, this is precisely the atmosphere one would hope for at home or in the classroom, no matter what is being taught.

It has been my experience that this accepting atmosphere, combined with the young poets' growing ease and familiarity with the world of words and frequent exposure to poetry by established writers will result in a new attitude toward literature. Once they have struggled with the medium themselves, children will become acutely aware of the frustrations and satisfactions all authors experience. Their appreciation of good writing develops because they know what the writer must go through to achieve it.

A boy from a "culturally deprived" neighborhood dashed to my desk one day with a poem he'd found by Emily Dickinson.

"She sweeps with many-colored brooms," he read. And then, with that feeling we all recognize when we've met something really fine, he added, "Jeez. I wish *I'd* thought of writing that."

Sky
The shimering sky
hold's every twinkling star
Every twinkling star
holds an avalanche of wishes

By Angie Miller

Words Are the Beginning

Words. All of our lives we live with words—spoken, written, read, heard. Words mold us, ove us, stop us, start us. We selom think much about them, and after years and years of using words, we have a tendency to employ them in pretty routineways. Because a bland, colorless way of expressing ourselves can take over at a surrisingly early age I believe it is essential that children be allowed to let their natural flair for imaginative thinking get a firm hold on their writing. Children should be encouraged to experience the work, the joy, the satisfaction of having written something that's true, beautiful, and imaginative.

Sherwood Anderson once wrote in an essay that "one works with words and one would like words that have a taste on the lips, that have a perfume to the nostrils, rattling words one can throw into a box and shake, making a sharp, jingling sound. . . ."

This attitude toward language is one that we need to develop in ourselves and in the children we teach. Its playfulness suggests a comfortable relationship between the writer and the tools of writing. Its selectivity suggests the writer's never ending but highly interesting task of discovering exactly the right word for this feeling, that sound, a movement, a color.

So, let's begin by asking the children to find some words to "throw into a box and shake."

Start with *fire*. Fire has a feel. What is the feeling of fire? *Hot* is the word we all think of first. But other words mean hot, too. Do you know any? What words mean *fire*? What words mean *burn*? What other words tell us something about a fire? Do any flowers make you think of fire? Any tastes? Red chili peppers? What smells like fire? What animal moves like a flame? What bird? What is the opposite of fire? Do you like the names of jewels? Are any jewels like fire?

See fire. What is burning? How does it look? Can you hear the fire? It makes sounds that mean *hot* and *fire* and *burn*. What are some sound words for fire?

We need color now. What color is the fire? Can you see it there behind your eyes? Write down the fiery scenes you can see in your mind.

As the children think of words, write them all on a chalkboard (or large piece of paper if you're working at home) where everyone can see them, until there is a tapestry of potential images. As your own imagination suggests ideas to you, ask for more and more words. You may also want to suggest that the children copy down the words that are on the chalkboard or paper in case the words are erased before the children are finished exploring for images.

Asking questions to draw out more and more vivid words works for very young writers, who are just beginning, and for older children and adults as well. There is something exciting and inspiring about a surface covered with potential poems. Your chalkboard or paper should shimmer with its fabric of words, words, and more words!

One September in a small city in northern California, a group of third graders wrote their first mind pictures after a preliminary session of putting a barrage of words on the chalkboard. Here are some results that came out of the word-shaking that day:

Crackle, s,s,s,s,s,s, red hot, orange, red.

—JOHN

A fire, crackle, blaze, help!

—NEIL

Red hot fire. People running and yelling
    and firetrucks coming.

—SHARON

The flames grow bigger and bigger. They
    crack!
And crack! As they burn the
    trees.

—RANDY

George, a sixth grader, wrote the following poem after fifteen minutes of thinking about fire:

Boiling steaming orange
The white wavers burn, scorch, crackle,
    roar, destroy, char,
and leave black singe.

—GEORGE, AGE 12

His vocabulary has grown since the days when he was eight years old. But he can write using the same idea starter—fire—that the eight-year-olds used.

Word exploration is rewarding in itself, whether an attempt is made to organize the words into recognizable poems or not. The images and sounds written during a word-shaking session form their own constellations of sound and color.

Words flew up onto the board one April morning when the sixth graders and I excitedly pointed out to each other that, after a long Minnesota winter, we were suddenly noticing the trees again. We all agreed that none of us had really "seen" those trees since the last leaves fell off sometime in late October.

My question to the children was, "Where have those trees been all this time? Why haven't we paid attention to the trees for so many months? Why do we notice them now? What has changed?"

Before they could answer, I challenged them to "think like a poet thinks. Give us answers that can't possibly be 'true,' in scientific terms, but that will put a new spin on the coming of spring."

The children agreed that the reason the trees had jumped back into our brains was the sudden appearance of a lacy film of green after months of a black and white and grey world. The task now was to put words on the board that would result in poem making. I like to get nifty verbs up on the board or on paper by asking for words that describe actions we can make with our eyes, with our neck, with our head, waist, hands, fingers, etc.

This brainstorming will generate words like point, blink, shake, bend, twist, grab. Architectural features of the room or of buildings are good—corner, floor, window, door, rooftops, hinge, ceiling—because these words will find themselves used in new ways as soon as they are seen in the company of all the other words. The same holds true of color words, and things that suggest particular colors, such as minerals, flower names, and birds.

That April morning, we went through lots of word playing, and when I asked, "Where have the trees been?" the word "closet" was offered. It was changed to "broom closet" when the poets saw it as part of the first line because "a broom closet would hold a tree. It is a tall, skinny closet. . . ." I asked for words that mean *spring* to them. The board began to fill up with the whole tapestry of ideas you can see here.

Here is the poem that resulted from playing around with this clutter of words:

APRIL
All winter long
I have kept the trees
in the broom closet
Now robins announce
the rain
Restless, the trees,
scratch at the locked
door
This key of thunder
lets them out
to sweep the open sky!

—GRADE SIX

This poem originally began with the words, "All winter I have kept the trees . . ." but the children decided that it didn't feel as endless as our winter had been. It was suggested that the word *long* be added. If you will read it both ways, you'll see that this simple addition makes the desired difference.

I asked that the poets put "I" somewhere in the poem, to give it the feeling of personal experience, even though we were planning to say some impossible things! The "key of thunder" image would never have come to mind if both words had not been on the board. This technique works because looking at the endless possibilities of combinations makes one's mind open up and begin to experiment!

I used this same page of words (with an overhead projector) with several other groups of children. Just for fun, I asked each of the groups to make up a poem with the word *loosen* at the beginning of three lines, and to put the word *let* at the beginning of the fourth line. In Missouri, a roomful of children wrote:

Dear Spring,
Loosen the emerald
leaf
Loosen the limestone
sky
Loosen the diamond
ice
Let the orchard color
flow.

—GRADES FOUR AND FIVE

Months later, back in Minnesota, I asked some fourth graders to use the idea of "night" for their poem. I was curious to see what these children would do, looking at the very same collection of words. They came up with this in just a few minutes of picking and choosing their favorite combinations:

Loosen a star
Loosen the moon
Loosen the light
Let it dance across
the sky
in the midnight air

—GRADE FOUR

You can see that if you had a notebook full of these motivating papers at hand for the children to use at will (copied off the board after a brainstorming session, or written on paper in the first place), the possibilities for imaginative language use are truly endless.

Here are the third graders again. Listen to their wordplaying with all sorts of topics:

SNAKE
I see him hit himself
over the rocks.

—THIRD-GRADE CHILD
WITH BEHAVIOR PROBLEMS

ANGER
When I am mad
I am steaming hot
and sparkles shoot
out of my eyes.

—JON, AGE 7

WIND
The wind howled.
It pecked on the
roof.
The wind blew.
It screamed
at my face.

—JEFF S.

SILENCE
All night
the moon floats in the puddle.
All day
clouds smother the bright sun.

After rain—
a rainbow
full of
pantomiming colors!

—BILL K., AGE 8

RAINY WEATHER
On a dark night
thunder slams.
Lightning winks
The house is asleep
I hear the unsteady
crutches of rain
hobbling across the roof.
I see silk thread
on my window
I fall asleep, listening.

—KARA, AGE 8

JOY
I am excited . . .
and sounds
come out of my mouth—
red and blue!

—MARCIA, AGE 7

SUMMER RAIN
I dream of
a cool wet meadow
after the storm.

The ground is a sponge,
and the sky is white and blue.
Look! A dove!

—CHAD, AGE 8

In the chapters that follow, you will read things written by children of all ages. Keep in mind that before young writers start a writing session, the same sort of mental word stretching described above should go on. Use it often for a surefire way to get the creative juices bubbling. I can just about guarantee an explosion of ideas and images on paper.

Brainstorming at home can take place at any time, of course, and I have found that the presence of food can trigger some far-out responses! You can ask the child, "How can we describe this fried egg? Look at it as though you have never see it before. What does the yolk remind you of? How about the white? What do the edges of the white part remind you of?"

If you have a pet, look at it with your child. Can you and your child describe how it moves?

There are no limits, as you can see, to the possibilities that exist all around us for creative expression. You will be able to think of dozens of opportunities that I cannot begin to list here. Something as ordinary as water pouring out of a faucet into a tub can generate exciting word pictures using sound, sight, texture. A stream of honey leaving the lip of a jar might bring an unexpected description from the child.

Try describing vegetables or fruit as people: Does this stalk of celery have a job? Who *is* this stalk of celery? What kind of a voice does it have? Does it have a particular kind of personality?

Ask your young poets to give personalities to the numbers from one to nine. You'll be surprised at their willing response to your weird request!

Explore different beginning words for poems. If left to themselves, many people, children and adults as well, will begin a piece of writing with *the*. Now there is nothing wrong with *the*—it is a useful and necessary word. But it gives the effect, sometimes, of a heavy, dull, clumpiness that can slow down an otherwise lively poem. So, every once in a while, it is a good idea to remind children—and ourselves—that the language is crammed with millions of words, none of them being *the*, all waiting for a chance to become the first word of a poem! Make a rule now and then, to be respected as rules for writing haiku and cinquain are respected: for one week no poem will allow itself to begin with *the*.

This rule might cause consternation at first. As you will see later in the book, a whole classroom of third graders once began their poems about the sun with "The sun . . ."; and "The sea . . ." appeared on many papers, too. It is not a crime to start a poem with *the*. But as children become more and more aware of the thrilling possibilities of language, they will find more vigorous ways to begin their poems.

A poem can begin with a questioning word. Who . . . ? What . . . ? When . . . ? Why . . . ? Did . . . ? How . . . ? If . . . then . . . ? Words like *when* and *where* can be used not only to ask questions but also to make statements: "When it rains . . ."; "Where lilies grow . . ."; "When time isn't clocked. . . ."

Try using words that end in -*ed*. *Blended, marked, blackened, pillowed, pointed, started* might all be good words to start a poem about fire, smoke, or some other topic. Let the children create a poem together.

What adverbs can the children think of? Suggest they start poems with some -*ly* adverbs: *lightly, sprightly, slowly, newly, brokenly, raggedly*. Or they can invent words, as Kelly does in her poem in the "Morning" chapter of this book. She used the word *sunly*; then she made up another word, *lemoned*, using it as a verb to tell us what the "morning sunly" did.

A poem's mood can be made more immediate and personal if the word *I* or *you* or *my* is used. Specific names of people, places, flowers, animals make a poem more interesting and more immediate.

Once you've introduced your children to these different ways of beginning poems and have collaborated on one or two poems, you can write first lines on the board or sheet of paper. If some children are excited about the possibility of using one or more of the lines in a poem of their own, that's fine. Those lines can then become the exclusive property of the children who choose them. Or the whole boardful can be fair game for all. In fact, it is often interesting to see in how many different directions a poem can go, given an identical first line. Either way is fine. Try them both.

Open up one of the books of poetry suggested in the bibliography at the end of this book and look at the ways in which its poems start. Read some first lines aloud to the children to see how they respond. Ask the children if they would have chosen the same first word. Why? Why not? What would be another choice for the first word? Another, another? Can they tell from the first line what the rest of the poem is going to be like?

If you begin this exploration of their language with the children, you'll find a comfortable relationship growing between them and their ability to handle the written word. Their attitude toward other poets—whether famous, published, or classmates—will develop into one of understanding and respect. They will begin to identify with the thought processes that take place inside a writer's head before a poem is written. Like the eight-year-old mentioned in the introduction, children will have a heartfelt appreciation of good writing, often accompanied by the fervent, "I wish I'd thought of writing that."

And when their own writing falls short in their own eyes, it will be because they have set some standards for themselves, based not on what the teacher likes, but on what they've come to recognize as effective, clear, and inventive use of language. This is what poetry is all about.

This book has two aims. First, it seeks to help you, to *urge* you to present children with endless opportunities for exploring their own language and for exploring ways that they can use that language to express their own ideas. Second, this book seeks to make you an appreciator of the lively things children can do with words. If these aims are fulfilled, your children will become both users and appreciators of the process writers everywhere have always employed in order to create life from words.

In this book we will look at writing about many different topics: people, animals, weather, oceans, the time of day. Of course, all of these topics and exercises could be used for stories as well as for poems. But story writing is another subject entirely and deserves a book of its own. The children's work reproduced in this book and the work your children produce from the ideas in this book will take the form of poetry, few words instead of many. Some of the chapters contain a few passages of short poetic prose dealing with the subject. These, too, demonstrate how children can creatively handle language. "In All Kinds of Weather" contains short prose weather myths written by third graders in conjunction with a science project. And those words will be a delight to our senses and to our sense of what writing creatively is all about.

I speak of the sea.
It crashes the land.
Smashing everything in its way.
In a funnel its cruel eyes look look for what?
A boat or person to drown
A dark sky appears.
The wind whirls the sea
Now its over
Now you see a blue sparkling sea

By Erin Vize
5-k

Sea Songs

Probably nothing in nature has been used quite so frequently for subject matter in poetry and prose as the sea. For those who live near the ocean, its moods, its sounds, its smells, and the creatures and plants beneath and around it all become part of their lives. For inland dwellers, the sea can be a far-off mystery to be deliciously imagined, vicariously enjoyed. All of the poems in thischapter, with one exception, were written by children in northwestern California or by Micronesian young people from the scattered islands in the western Pacific.

The Micronesian students spoke and wrote English as a foreign language, so their problems of self-expression were similar to those of native English speakers eight or nine years old. We worked together in the same way I worked with other students. We began by filling a chalkboard with words and images. Then we spun off into associations that resulted from continual pulling out of words and questioning their meanings.

Begin with the sounds of the sea. Think about the way waves move toward the shore. See how they build and build into a long curve. See and hear that curve curl over and strike the land. Are the waves strong? Are they heavy? What sound does that great volume of water make when it reaches the shore? What word conveys that sound? What else makes such a noise?

Here are some third graders' impressions of the sounds made by waves:

> The sea roars.
> It is silver,
> and it reflects
> on ocean liners.
>
> —CHRIS, AGE 8

> When thunder comes,
> the sea sounds
> like roaring tigers.
> It races to shore
> and races back.
> It looks like

green, blue, and white
flowers.

—DELAYNE, AGE 8

"There are many noises in the sea," eight-year-old Diana
wrote, and she added:

The sea roars like lions
all through the day.

Another child hears a different kind of sound at the sea's
edge:

Sounds of the sea gulls
lead the way
to the sea—

—MARLENE, AGE 10

Listen to the almost deafening sound as Irene repeats *roaring*
in her poem:

The sea is sometimes fearful
and sometimes gentle.
But the sea sometimes has visitors
that come to join the roaring party
of the sea.
They are dressed in rainbow colors.
And the roaring breakers
come breaking up
the roaring party.

—IRENE, AGE 9

The main images of these poems convey the sea through its sounds. They contain words that sound like the sounds the sea makes.

Poets often use the sounds within words to convey a particular image. Say these words aloud and listen to the sounds they make: *crack, splat, smack, glitter, break, slap.* The consonants *t, k,* hard *c* make these words sound harsh. The short vowel sounds, in all but *break,* help evoke a feeling of quick motion. They can speed up the action of a poem and sometimes harden it.

But there are other words that we naturally linger over: *roll, roar, pound, smash, boom.* Long vowel sounds, combination sounds like *ou,* and softer consonants, especially the *sh* sound, contribute to a feeling of slowness. These words can slow down the action of a poem and make us aware of bigness, lengthiness, power. Compare the sounds in "heavy boulders" with the sounds in "little pebbles." See how much more quickly the words "little pebbles" move.

In this next poem, Neil uses drawn-out words like *booming, crashes,* and *looms* to suggest a feeling of bigness and power. Notice how he takes his time before he lets you see that his word portrait of the sea is a night scene:

The sea is like a booming drum.
It crashes the salt water
against the reflection of the light
from the lighthouse
that looms
against the cliffs
and guides the ships
home.

—Neil, age 8

After a morning of experimenting with the effect sounds have on the pace of a poem, Linda wrote the following poem to show a quiet scene and a smooth night sea:

The sea is soft at night,
and shines
like gold.
The moon shines
like a silver dish.

—LINDA, AGE 9

Read the poem aloud. It is almost impossible to rush this poem. We seem to want to stay with words like *soft, night, shines, gold, moon, silver.* Linda has achieved the effect she wishes by her choice of words and by the way those words sound. Creating word images depends on listening with the inner ear as well as seeing with the mind's eye.

The sea's bouncing.
It jumps and storms and falls—
The waves look white as paper
and it sucks the sands from the shore.
And the sea
is mighty terrific!

—TOM, AGE 9

The most startling image in this poem is the "sea's bouncing." *Bouncing* is a good example of the kind of unusual and descriptive movement word that can come from the word-shaking sessions at the chalkboard.

Look at the glorious words that evoke water's qualities in the next poem. Joni makes us *see* and *hear* water!

I follow
silky minnows
under transparent
folds.
I hold
an umbrella-backed
turtle into the
sparkling sun.
I see wild water
shattering over
calm stones.
I hear
sheets of water
slapping against
the sand.

—JONI, AGE 11

There are only three quiet images in this poem. What are they?

A Micronesian student also writes of the opposite moods of the familiar sea. She personifies the sea and the wind as they meet each other:

> He is full of wonders . . .
> He is so strange that he can lift
> The biggest ship ever built,
> But he can't lift the smallest stone
> Ever found.
> He is at peace only
> When the wind
> Is being easy on him.
>
> When Wind comes along
> Struggling and blowing hard,
> He, too, struggles hard,
> Making lots of noises.
>
> When Wind sympathetically draws himself
> Somewhere in a corner
> of the skies,
> He becomes so glassily smooth
> that I, a curious girl,
> Wish to walk in high-heeled shoes
> on his surface
> And watch the wondrous lives
> beneath me.
>
> —MARIA R., AGE 17

Notice how the word *struggle* shows the interaction between the sea and the wind. And then suddenly we see the struggle end; we see an absolutely calm, unmoving surface. The surface is "glassily smooth," calm and steady enough to be walked on "in high-heeled shoes."

The incongruity of the sea's being able to lift the "biggest ship ever built" but unable to lift the "smallest stone ever found" tells us something about the physical properties of the sea. It's the common physical phenomenon, water displacement, which we have all puzzled over, stated in a wonderfully fresh way. These images are what makes this poem work so well.

David spoke of the sea as "a hill." In this next poem, Masaharu, a Micronesian student, uses that same image. He repeats the phrase "rolling hills of waves" and the words *foam* and *roll* to achieve the feeling of the forward and backward, onrush and retreat, motion of endless waves:

When your rolling hills of waves break
on the reef, tops are concealed by snow.
Yet, what I see is not snow, but foam,
and the foam I see is no longer foam,
but again,
the rolling hills of waves.

When the dancing waves roll and roll,
crushed and broken by the reef,
I shall hear your calls in rhythm.
But when I call for you,
You will not hear me,
for my voice shall drown
in the roaring music
of the dark blue sea.

—MASAHARU, AGE 17

THE SEA
The breakers
like a mountain range
put into motion,
like an angry beast.

Toward the isle,
white horses
swept ashore.

—FABYAN, EARLY 20S

Jerry imagined a fish breaking through the water's surface:

The sea shines like crystals,
And when a fish jumps
Out of the water,
It breaks crystals,
One at a time.

—JERRY, AGE 8

Can you see those shiny crystals, harder and more fragile than you might expect water to be? Can you see them forming and breaking "one at a time"? Those last four words give a slow-motion effect that prints, on our minds, the image of the fish's thrust, the water breaking apart, and the crystal beads breaking as we watch.

Colors come and go over the surface of the water, changing it from moment to moment, season to season. What makes the ocean's color? Let's name some of the colors we see in the sea. What makes the water blue? What is another word for blue? Another? Name other things that are blue. Can you compare the sea with these other blue things?

What about green? What else is green? Are there green gems?

What are their names? Does a drop of green water have anything in common with a green gem? If you drop a big green jewel, it might break. What are some words that mean *break*? Can these words be used to describe water breaking against the shore?

What makes the ocean white? We saw in Tom's poem that "the waves look white as paper." Think of some other white things. Mike's poem needs some comparisons to make it more interesting. What could he have used to let us see those gray whitecaps more clearly?

> The sea is blue when it is calm.
> But, when it is stormy, it is white,
> And gray whitecaps appear.
>
> —MIKE, AGE 8

Are there some pure white things in nature that could be compared with the whitecaps on waves? Is snow a good comparison? Why? Think of a kind of fabric that is often white and may remind you of foam. Can we see a lacy edge to a wave?

When is the sea gray? Can the sea be gray and calm? If you imagine a calm, gray sea, can you compare it with something else that is smooth and dull? Name some gray things, metals, fabrics. Are there fabrics that could be used to describe the mist, the fog, or the rain-blurred skies above the sea? Can you compare the gray sea with an animal? Stretch your mind and see things you have not seen before.

Donna's poem is lively because of the carefully chosen words, especially the color image she uses:

> The sea is as green
> as cat's eyes!
> The waves are crashing
> against the rocks

and the waves rock little fish
and move things.

—DONNA, AGE 8

The main technique I used was to draw out live, descriptive words about the ocean. You might also explore the feel of the water, the temperature, the salt, the sand. Or use any other aspect of the sea that strikes you or the children.

In her poem, Eva wants us to experience the coldness of the sea:

The sea is as cold as a snowflake,
Its shining waves go by;
And when I think of a snowflake,
I think of the sea, with a sigh.

—EVA, AGE 8

In another poem emphasizing the temperature of the water, Marcia repeats *cool* in order to let us feel this special quality of her sea:

> The ship in the cool sea,
> The fish in the cool sea,
> The water is a-splashing
> And a-dashing
> Against a thunder ship.

—MARCIA, AGE 10

Water in general is a fascinating subject for poetry. If you feel too removed from the ocean, use a river, lake, puddle, or pond for subject matter. What do all bodies of water have in common? How are they different? You could go on and on, writing about water.

In Wendy's poem, the images allow us to see water moving, and water as "a transparent sheet." The water changes color as we read, and goes from wild to tame:

> Water:
> swishing whirlpool
> bubbles all around.
> Water:
> gleams in the moonlight
> a transparent sheet.
> Water:
> aqua,
> green, blue—
> blueaquagreen!
> Water:
> rippling liquid
> foamy on its banks
> wild though tame.

Water:
you can see it
a mirror
a sheet of glass
sparkling diamonds.

—WENDY, AGE 12

Nita manages to let us see, hear, and feel the water. In her poem the water braids "between rocks"—something we will all remember the next time we are near a flowing stream!

Hear the water sing,
hear the water chuckle.
See the water braiding between
rocks,
see the water flip and toss.
Feel the water run through your
fingers like silk.
Feel the water's lizards, fish
and whales.
Can you feel it?
Tell me.
Can you hear the waters whisper?

—NITA, AGE 10

And who can ever forget, once we've read it, the "wrinkled blue ribbon" that James has conjured up for us? This image is accurate and miraculous!

RIVER
The flowing water
is a wrinkled

blue ribbon that
someone
cannot straighten
out.

—JAMES, AGE 10

How can words give the feeling of the push and pull of the waves? Steven thought of give-and-take as an image that might work. When he read this poem to us, the whole fifth grade class applauded!

THE SEA
White pillows
Come crashing
To rocky shores!
Leave something
Take something

To their Mother the Moon
They give diamonds
Take emeralds
Return emeralds
Take diamonds

Continually on chains
Made of
Sapphire

—STEVEN, AGE 10

We talked about the fact that tides come in and go out because of the moon's influence. Look at how Traci imagines the moon pulling the sea. Steven could see sapphire chains. Traci gives us a black velvet ribbon. Both images are spectacular.

Here come the waves
flowing and sliding
caught
in seaweed
The silky moon pulls the sea
in with a black velvet ribbon

—TRACI, AGE 10

It occurred to me, when I had finished reading their sea poems to them, to ask the California children how many had actually been to the beaches of the cold northern coast. To my astonishment, only a handful had seen the ocean. Yet through their imaginations, perhaps with the aid of pictures they'd seen or facts they knew about the sea, they were able to evoke the ocean-ness, the sea-flavor word pictures we accept as true in the best, the poetic, sense.

Cinquain

Mourning
a love gone by
he lives on a park bench
a mansion floats into his
dream
at night.

by Seth - 11

Cinquain: Two, Four, Six, Eight, Two

After early word experiments, I have sometimes found it to be a satisfying next step to work with the cinquain form. Cinquains were invented years ago by Adelaide Crapsey, an American poet who studied Japanese haiku.

Crapsey developed the form for a five-line poem in which the first line has two syllables, the second line has four, the third line

has six, the fourth line has eight, and the fifth line ends the poem
with two syllables. In her skilled poet's hands the cinquain became a subtle, sophisticated form.

TRIAD*
These be
Three silent things:
The falling snow . . . the hour
Before the dawn . . . the mouth of one
Just dead.

—ADELAIDE CRAPSEY

Writing in a form with a specified number of syllables demon-
strates to children that much can be said in a few words. The syllable count forces writers to choose their words more carefully. A
real mind stretching occurs as the poet searches for the right
word with the right number of syllables.

The only caution I would offer at this point is that you urge
children to continue to search for just the right word. They
should not fall into either of these cinquain traps: choosing a
word just because it has a certain number of syllables, or adding
inessential articles or adjectives to fill out the syllable count. The
challenge in writing a cinquain is to find vivid words to express
the writer's thoughts within the five-line form.

Writing cinquains is a logical first step to writing haiku, a more
complicated poetic form discussed in the next chapter. A haiku,
with seventeen syllables, requires further comprehension of
meaning and greater care in choosing words.

To introduce the cinquain, I first tell the children that we're going to write a poem together, that it will have five lines, and that

---

* From _Verse_ by Adelaide Crapsey, Alfred A. Knopf, Inc., New York, 1938.
Reprinted with permission of the publisher.

each line will have a certain number of syllables in it. I tell them the name *cinquain* and explain its form. Then I show them the syllable count on the chalkboard like this:

2

4

6

8

2

I suggest that they write the numbers on a piece of paper. Then, as we work out a couple of cinquains using ideas from all the children, they write down the words for each line.

When my children did this in our home, we thumb-tacked a big piece of paper onto a cutting board and leaned it against the back of a chair seat. Be inventive! How about magnets to hold the paper on the fridge?

One afternoon I was invited to work with some sixth graders who had had little writing experience of the kind we've been discussing. After talking about the power of words, we decided to think about the idea of a storm. First we filled the chalkboard with storm words. What does a storm look like? What color is it? What does it sound like? What instrument in an orchestra sounds like a storm? What does a storm smell like? What does the air feel like right before and after a storm? We filled the chalkboard with words and I introduced the cinquain. The children decided on the two-syllable word *thunder* for the first word.

Now the cinquain-to-be on the chalkboard looked like this:

2 Thunder

4

6

8

2

What should the four-syllable line say? "Lightning flashes" was the unanimous choice, and the cinquain continued:

2 Thunder
4 Lightning flashes
6
8
2

Now for a six-syllable line, I encouraged, warning about careful syllable counting. One of the girls suggested a line. We can see how the poem developed:

2 Thunder
4 Lightning flashes
6 Jagged streaks, cymbal strikes
8
2

The word *cymbal* was one of the chalkboard words suggested in response to the question, "What instrument of an orchestra reminds you of a storm?"

The eight-syllable line seems incredibly long to children; it has acres of room compared to the two-syllable first line. See how this fourth line rolls along:

2 Thunder
4 Lightning flashes
6 Jagged streaks, cymbal strikes

8 Howling organ—wind bellowing

2

And now we are at the end, in need of a two-syllable line that will clinch the poem. This last line can have an interesting effect on the reader. It brings a finality to the poem in one of several ways. The two beats can sound hollow, like the voice of doom, the end. Adelaide Crapsey's line, "Just dead," gives that feeling. Or they can be a frantic cry or a neat summing up; or they can be humorous, as we'll see in some of the other cinquains in this chapter.

Following some lively debate and deliberation, we finally agreed that our joint-effort poem would look like this:

2 Thunder!
4 Lightning flashes—
6 Jagged streaks, cymbal strikes,
8 Howling organ—wind bellowing.
2 Help me!

We added punctuation marks to make the poem clearer. This completed our cinquain, a strong statement about a storm.

Writing one or more cinquains as a group seems to motivate individual effort. As children begin their own cinquains, remind them that the number at the beginning of each line is there to indicate how many syllables they should have in that line.

In order to help the children answer the what-shall-I-write-about question, I like to have a mystery box ready, filled with slips of folded paper, each containing an idea for a poem. These poem starters can be nouns, subjects for poems, words they might use in the poem, action verbs that might suggest a poem, anything that might set their imaginations on fire.

Each child reaches into the box and chooses his or her own slip. I am careful to point out that this slip of paper is a thought starter only. If children have their own ideas, they are free to use them.

Before the children begin writing, review some of the exciting words that can begin a poem: the question words, *who, what, why, where, when;* the action words. Encourage the children to brainstorm for themselves, using their idea starters, to think of colors, shapes, smells, in the same way they would search as a group for words to fill the chalkboard on a given topic.

In the following poems, the title is usually the starter word or idea from the mystery box:

STORM
It bangs
and slams the sky-door
shut. It bends the trees
and sends bright lights curling in
the sky.

—FIRST-GRADE CLASS

SPIDER WEB
Morning,
Glistening in sun,
Cool breezes blow on webs,
Fly trapped in the colors of it,
No more.

—ELIZABETH, AGE 11

SPIDER WEB
Knitting,
Weaving, testing,
Calculating. Feeling

her trap to tangle victims in:
Deadly.

—GEORGE, AGE 12

THE STORM
Thunder!
Lightning flashing!
Black moonless, starless sky;
Thunder rolling like a bass drum.
The storm.

—STANLEY, AGE 11

Stanley's mystery slip contained the same topic the class had chosen for its poem. However, even though he uses some of the same words, notice how he focuses on different sights and sounds.

The people in the writers' lives make good subjects for cinquains:

MY BROTHER
Tony,
My dumb brother.
Inconsiderate, too;
Menace of Atlanta, Georgia:
Brother!

—STANLEY, AGE 11

Stanley told us that the final word was pronounced bro-*ther*, giving his cinquain a humorous twist.

All sorts of people can be inspiration for cinquains (and other poems). So put some names in your mystery box; use real people, folk heroes, and silly strange names that make the writers want to describe the person who owns that name.

Historical figures, real or legendary, as well as people in the writers' lives make good subjects for cinquains:

PAUL REVERE
He rode
To warn people
That the Britishers came
To rob, kill, and squash the people.
He rode.

—RUTHIE, AGE 10

CHARLES DE GAULLE
Big nose,
Talks with a roar,
Six feet five, quite alive,
Perfect image of Frankenstein.
Bye, France!

—ELLEN, AGE 11

MATT DILLON
Dillon,
Tall as the West,
Marshall of Dodge City,
Keeper of law and order—
Big man.

—PHILIP, AGE 11

In a poem we are always looking for fresh language, a new way to say something. Philip's image of Matt Dillon as "Tall as the West" is a good one.

When Mike picked "Jack and Jill" from the mystery box, neither he nor the class expected the poem that resulted.

JACK AND JILL
Water,
Well on a hill.
A gay group of children
Sliding down a hill, thinking death—
Poor kids!

—MIKE, AGE 11

The circus has an endless supply of poem starters just waiting
to be used. Put some circus ideas on slips of paper in your mystery box. They never fail:

THE CLOWN
Funny—
He makes me laugh,
Waddling Mr. Clown
When you ride in a ring car,
HA HA!

—TINA, AGE 12

Animating the inanimate is still another way to make an ordinary idea come to life, a fresh way of stating something we all
may have thought about:

MORNING
Morning
Comes on the night
like a robber stealing
something precious from a big house.
Morning.

—ELLEN, AGE 11

This image catches our attention, for it reverses the way poets have often depicted morning and evening. Evening in poems has been referred to as stealing away the day. But, here, morning is compared to a thief, stealing the dark jewels of night.

This quiet scene is a picture of an animal at night:

SWAN
Moonlight
A swan is still,
He lifts his graceful head
And slowly descends in the light . . .
Gone now.

—TINA, AGE 12

TIGHTROPE WALKER
Brave man
On a high wire
Above the spellbound crowd.
Like a spider on its silk web,
He glides.

—JOSEPH, AGE 13

Cinquains that begin with *-ing* words can present powerful pictures. In the following poem, Bert uses strong words:

RACE
Screeching!
Crash violently
Cars burn. Rubber! Smash! BAM
Car explodes violently—AAH
But wait . . .

—BERT, AGE 11

This is a good example of the surprise ending, the twist the last line can give a cinquain. What really happened? Was there a crash? Why wait?

A good *-ing* word starts us off with the feeling of flight in this next poem:

EAGLE
Soaring,
Swooping down from
High on the mountain tops,
Catching animals from the air.
Eagles.

—DAVE, AGE 11

The three action words—*soaring*, *swooping*, and *catching*—combined with the long vowel sounds in the poem give us a very distinct picture of the majestic eagle.

By this time it must be obvious that ideas for cinquains, like ideas for any other kind of imaginative writing, exist everywhere. One is limited only by the number of lines and the syllable count. Stretch your minds and imaginations with words, and the form and syllable counting will only make your expressions more interesting.

Turn the children loose with 2-4-6-8-2. Good things will happen. And on to haiku.

Reddish rhubarb stems
Sprout among patches of snow
In the cool spring air

Leslie

Haiku

What Is Haiku?

After children have become accustomed to the restrictions of cinquain and to its delightful possibilities, they can tackle the even more restrictive haiku form.

Haiku is a Japanese form of poetry that calls for seventeen syllables in three lines. The lines have syllable counts of five, seven, and five. Three other general rules must also be followed if the writer's end result is to be a genuine haiku.

First, a haiku must *refer in some way to nature.* The poem doesn't have to be about nature, but there must be a nature clue or reference included in it.

The second requirement for writing haiku is that the poem should *refer to a particular event as it is presently taking place.* The haiku writer must focus on a specific occurrence. (A robin eating a worm is an immediate, specific occurrence; the return of spring is not.) Nor can the specific event be described in the past tense. Haiku uses only *now* words!

Using a particular event is essential to writing haiku, according to Harold G. Henderson in his excellent book *Haiku in English.* "The idea is so fundamental in Japanese haiku," says Henderson, "that we do not believe any poet attempting to write haiku in English can ignore it and still write haiku." Generalizations do not belong in haiku.

Rule three requires that the haiku *suggest to the reader the emotions the poet feels* while describing the particular event.

Although some practitioners of haiku in English don't feel bound by these rules, I find that most people—and especially beginners—do their best work in this strict form. Like the writer of haiku in Japanese, the English-speaking haiku poet must cope with the limitations imposed by the seventeen syllables. The poet's words must therefore be carefully chosen, and the poetic idea must be focused and distilled into a clear expression of the original thought. The experience is valuable for any writer at any age.

In this chapter, we will be talking about haiku in which the poet objectively *observes* a relationship between separate things. Even though the poet hints at or expresses an emotion about what is being observed, he or she is essentially an outside ob server, not a part of what is being observed. Haiku that depends on visual impressions is sometimes called picture haiku. The challenge is to make these delicate pictures as clear as one can, using only the seventeen syllables.

Look at the comparisons in this poem by Bashō, a Japanese writer (1644–1694).* In the original Japanese, this haiku followed the 5-7-5 format, but Henderson, the translator, has chosen not to follow that form in his rendition:

On a withered branch
a crow has settled—
autumn nightfall.

Can you see the withered branch, night coming, and the small crow silhouetted against the autumn sky? Is there a suggestion of the poet's emotions in this poem? What might they be?

Objective haiku also makes use of other senses besides sight. Here is a poem by Anne Rutherford from the book *Borrowed Water: A Book of American Haiku.*†

South-bound roaring past
splintering the night with sound—
listen! a cricket.

To show us a night scene, the poet compares two sounds. Do you hear the train shattering the night? Do you then hear the soft night sound of the cricket? In the following poem, a combination of two senses is used:

* From *An Introduction to Haiku* by Harold G. Henderson. Copyright© 1958 by Harold G. Henderson. Used by permission of Doubleday & Company, Inc.
† From *Borrowed Water: A Book of American Haiku* by the Los Altos Writers Roundtable, Charles V. Tuttle, Co., Rutland, Vt., 1966, page 79. Reprinted with permission of the publisher.

Reddish rhubarb stems
   sprout among patches of snow
    In the cool spring air.

                  —LESLIE M., AGE 11

This poem shows us an early spring scene with rhubarb leaves just beginning to sprout and patches of snow on the ground. We see the leaves and the snow; we feel the cool air.

Leslie wrote this poem, too:

When the warm sun shines,
Little buds shoot up among
Whitened, stiff cornstalks.

Is it haiku? Ask yourself, "Does it describe a *particular* event, or is it a description of something that happens generally in spring?" Unlike Leslie's first poem, this one is a generalization and therefore not strictly haiku.

Perhaps you can rewrite it to make it a description of a particular event. How could this be done? "Whitened stiff cornstalks" does have the clarity of an event seen *now*. Maybe what is needed is a more definite picture in lines one and two. We need to experience what is happening *here* and at *this* moment. Would naming the kind of "little buds" help? Try some variations and see for yourself.

How to Begin

We have already placed much emphasis on wordplay as a way to begin writing poems. Wordplay is important in writing any poem. But in a strict form such as haiku and cinquain, in which the writer is limited to a certain number of syllables and the right word must be found, wordplay can be even more beneficial.

I've found that a good way to help children start writing haiku is to have a few sessions with ideas going up on the chalkboard or paper and all the children contributing to the work at hand.

To begin, I put a five-syllable first line on the chalkboard and ask the children to compose the second and third lines. This generates interest immediately. Everyone can contribute to the poem and can have a chance to try something new without the frustration of having to work out the whole poem alone.

Take a look at this five-syllable first line:

Feet squeaking on snow.

I wrote this haiku line on the board and asked the children to complete it, keeping in mind the following requirements: let us know somehow that it is almost dark outside and that the poet, while walking along, is either thinking about or actually seeing supper being prepared. I find that setting certain requirements like these sharpens the children's awareness of what words can do.

A different set of requirements to go with the same first line could have been: in lines two and three, let us know that it is a clear, cold, sunlit day in January and that the poet, while walking toward the skating rink, is aware of sharp blue shadows on snow.

If you will stop right this minute and try writing two haiku with the different sets of requirements in mind, you will see how different the word pictures will be.

After the children have suggested lines for the group haiku, I ask them each to write a poem individually. Here are some haiku that resulted from the original first line:

Feet squeaking on snow.
　Breathing in all the night air
　　The scent of supper.

　　　　　　　　　　　—JENNIFER B., AGE 13

Feet squeaking on snow.
　When lights begin to shine bright—
　　Hot, steaming supper.

　　　　　　　　　　　—TINA, AGE 12

Feet squeaking on snow.
　The street lights have just flicked on—
　　Clattering of spoons.

　　　　　　　　　　　—RITA, AGE 10

Rita had a terrible time trying to get the clue about supper into her poem. I think you'll agree that her solution is a marvelous one. The two fine words *flicked* and *clattering* show that earlier practice with wordplay certainly paid off for Rita.

Debbie found herself with two poems:

Feet squeaking on snow.
　Just can't wait for supper—mmm—
　　Shadow by moonlight.

This is her second poem:

Feet squeaking on snow.
　The strong night wind pushing you—
　　toward the scent of food.

　　　　　　　　　　　—DEBBIE, AGE 13

When Debbie read these aloud, the children felt that neither was quite right. Line two in the first poem sounded "blah" to them; line three in the second poem seemed "boring for a haiku." After some hotly debated suggestions, Debbie came up with the obvious answer:

> Feet squeaking on snow.
>> The strong night wind pushing you . . .
>>> Shadow by moonlight.

She sacrificed the supper clue but combined the best of the two poems to come up with a poem that pleased everyone.

Joseph reported that he had "messed around" with my suggested first line and just couldn't come up with a poem he liked. So he wrote his own first line and the following poem:

> The dim winter light—
>> Peering through steaming windows
>>> With hot food ready.
>>>> —JOSEPH, AGE 13

Joseph didn't use the same first line that everyone else did, but obviously the line made him think about what he could put into a poem. He did fulfill the other requirements. He explained that the dash after *light* indicates a "sort of stop" and that someone is inside peering out through a steaming window. Joseph felt that no punctuation at the end of the first line would make us think the winter light was doing the peering. What do you think?

I had some fourteen-year-old students suggest some first lines. They came up with these: The pond is stagnant, Winter's proudest crown, Reflections in glass, Children in the rain.

And here are some of the poems that these first lines suggested:

Winter's proudest crown
    Birch trees dotting the landscape
    With a rust mantle.

—CHRIS, AGE 14

Reflections in glass—
    Sunrise flowing into it
    And silence throughout.

—CAROLINE, AGE 14

Children in the rain—
    The sound of many horses?
    It's only small Jill . . .

—CAROLINE, AGE 14

Of the three, "Children in the rain—" is the best haiku. It shows us
something about the weather. We know that the poet, hearing a
lot of noise, is surprised that only one child is making the noise.

Could the other poems be improved by working comparisons
into them? Would using more specific words be any help? Try
your hand at adding twelve syllables to each of the suggested first
lines. See how well you do. You will be much more effective as a
teacher of haiku if you've had the fun and frustration of tackling
the form yourself.

A variation of the mystery box technique can be used for the
first five-syllable lines of a haiku. Keep a box or jar filled with a
supply of first lines, handy for the taking when children need them.

Since a haiku describes a particular event, you can also encourage the children to jot down notes on their own experiences
and the things that happen around them. They should include details about plants, animals, and other things in their everyday

lives. They can then go back to these notes when they need subject material.

There is another effective way to generate interest in writing haiku. In *An Introduction to Haiku*, Harold G. Henderson has given us his translations of original Japanese haiku. For each freely translated poem, he also presents the original haiku and his literal translation of each Japanese word.

I have found that it intrigues haiku writers to be given only this literal translation and to become the original writer of the haiku. I ask the student to try to get inside the mind of the Japanese writer who composed the poem so long ago and to write a haiku that will mirror the idea of the original writer. After the students write and read their poems, I put Henderson's professional one on the chalkboard so they can see how their work compares with his.

Here is an example of the way this works. First, the literal English translation from the Japanese is given to the children.

Sky | too | earth | too | are-not | only | snow
falls-ceaselessly

This is how some children expressed the thought of the writer:

Snow keeps falling
   Everything has vanished now.
     Where did it all go?

—RITA, AGE 10

Ice encrusts our house
   Neither sky nor earth are ours.
     Snow is our kingdom.

—ANN V., AGE 14

Earth has disappeared
　　Only snow is there falling,
　　　　falling ceaselessly.
　　　　　　　　　　—CHARLOTTE F., AGE 14

This example of literal Japanese intrigues children:

Snake I fleeing I me I had I looked-at I eyes'
grass-in remain

If one gets inside the original writer's mind, what does one find?
What exactly did the long ago Japanese writer think about this
particular snake? Where does the word *eyes* fit in? What does the
poet want you to feel about the eyes? Think about this snake.
How is it moving? Where is it? Does this interpretation say it as
you might say it yourself?

A snake looked at me—
　　then fled, but the hostile eyes
　　　　remained in the grass.
　　　　　　　　　　—LISA, AGE 14

Or this one?

Warm summer night out.
　　Snake slithers by the side-walk
　　　　Eyes still watching me.
　　　　　　　　　　—DEBBIE, AGE 13

Debbie's snake seems to live in the city.
　　Before you peek at the poems this next literal translation inspired, try writing a haiku yourself.

Distant-mountains' | eye-jewels | in | reflect
dragonfly

One group of children looked hard at a large color photograph
of a dragonfly, noting its separate parts and its color. Then, remembering dragonflies each had seen in the long past summer,
they wrote these poems. Rita added a color word to her picture.

Aquamarine wings—
    the dragonfly's eyes reflect
      mountains far away.

                —RITA, AGE 10

And Jennifer imagined many dragonflies.

Swarms of dragonflies
    their jewel eyes reflecting
    On the tall mountain.

            —JENNIFER, AGE 13

As you can imagine, that word *on* in line three was loudly criti-
cized. Jennifer countered with the argument that she needed five
syllables and was stuck otherwise. Someone suggested that if she
dropped the word *on* and settled for sixteen syllables, the poem
would make sense. The children felt the sense of the haiku was
more important than holding to seventeen syllables. To everyone's relief, Jennifer agreed.

    Joseph had two variations, both of them delightful. Which do
you prefer?

Pretty dragonfly,
    with jewels for eyes you fly
    and reflect mountains.

With jewel-like wings
   you fly with mirrors for eyes
      reflecting mountains.

                       —JOSEPH, AGE 13

This next literal translation was presented to a group of ninth grade girls whose ages ranged from thirteen to fifteen. Of all the Japanese poems, this one elicited the most enthusiastic response from them:

Spring-rain | grove | to | get-blown | thrown-
away-letter

According to Henderson, "A Japanese letter would be written on a single long sheet of flexible paper." I mentioned this to the students and asked them to picture the rainy scene and to think of reasons why there might be a discarded letter in the grove. Without exception, the girls in the class all came to the same conclusion.

The ink weaves red paths
   I stand here in wet silence
      The letter is gone—

                    —JULIE E., AGE 15

This next haiku sneaked by with six syllables in the last line. I included it here because of its wistful tone of resignation. Can you think of a way to change the last line to fit the format while retaining the tone of the poem?

It was raining hard
   When the wind blew his letter.
      It often rains in spring . . .

                 —BONNIE M., AGE 14

Poor lonely letter—
　All alone it bears the rain
　　Good-bye love. Good-bye.

　　　　　　　　　　—JACQUELINE, AGE 14

To those ninth graders, it was obviously a love letter. Henderson's version seems quite matter-of-fact in comparison:

SPRING RAIN
Rain on a spring day:
　to the grove is blown a letter
　　someone threw away.

All of the following were written by ninth graders, using the literal translations that appear above them:

Eleven-riders | faces | even | not-swing
blown-snow

Eleven riders'
　Swarthy faces not even
　　swinging from blown snow.

　　　　　　　　　　—ANN V., AGE 14

Caged-bird | butterflies | envy | eye-expression

The caged yellow bird
　envies the spring butterflies'
　　remorseless freedom.

　　　　　　　　　　—KATHRYN, AGE 14

Poor lonely caged bird
   watches the free butterfly
      through the metal bars.

                    —GAIL, AGE 14

High I noon I reed-sparrows I save-for I river's
sound I even I is-not

High noon brings calmness
   although reed sparrows still fly—
      Even the river sleeps.

                  —CHARLOTTE, AGE 14

With high noon, the bird
   coming to the river's edge
      listens to the sound—

                  —PATTI, AGE 14

Harold Henderson's book *Introduction to Haiku* contains his translations of over 300 haiku, with the original Japanese and the English literal translation. I strongly urge you to buy a copy. The book is a delight, and the literal translations are a never-ending challenge for haiku writers. Until you do own your copy, use this additional list of literal translations:

Winds I to I ask I which I first-ly I falling
tree-leaf

Butterflies' I lovingly-follow I flower-wreath
coffin's I top

People I go-home I afterward
be-dark

Moon I one-circle I stars I un-numbered I sky
dark I green

Short I night I shallows-in I remaining I moon
one-part

Become a haiku writer by beginning with these starters. Then try
them with the children.

Lead into Gold, Haiku's Alchemy

Why have we devoted so many pages to haiku? What can come
from the writing of seventeen-syllable, three-line verse? Why
should you spend a lot of time getting children to write in this
specific form? Why introduce haiku at all? The answer becomes
obvious if we examine the writing of children before and after
they have worked with haiku.

Compare the two efforts that Tina made to describe playing in
the snow. This is the first:

Playing all day—
Running and jumping in snow
Laughing all day
Even eating snow
But still having fun.

And this is the second:

Speeding down the hill
White soft snow higher than me.
Where are my mittens?

—TINA, AGE 14

In the first poem there is a loose generality of expression that seems bland and ordinary. In the haiku version, tautness and control are evident.

Here is another example. Joe, an eighth grader, was looking at an American history book, *This Fabulous Century* (Time-Life Books). He was especially taken with a section on old funny papers. The first thing he wrote expressed his feelings like this.

Me and my brother finally get the funnies. I grab Flash to see if he kills the Monster and saves the princess. But he's captured by the mad doctor Zin and is held by a secret force that Doctor Zin invented. Shucks! Got to wait till tomorrow to find out, doggonit.

When Joe used the same nostalgic pages for an idea starter to write haiku, here is what he wrote:

WAY BACK WHEN
Wonder what happened
    To Flash Gordon and Tarzan—
        and sunny Sundays.

—JOE, AGE 13

As you can see, this poem ignores two of the rules for haiku. It does not have a nature clue, nor does it describe something happening right now. However, its seventeen syllables crystallize Joe's thoughts. Joe commented that while writing the haiku he was aware for the first time of how un-funny the so-called funnies of the 1970s had become. The unexpected nostalgia of this thirteen-year-old came out in his haiku. And the other children in the group agreed that this haiku really said something to them. Jennifer felt it was "sad, but in a way I can't explain."

Over the years, I have found that haiku has a strong effect

upon the writing of young people. Others have also found this to be true, as can be seen from this quote taken from *Borrowed Water: A Book of American Haiku.* "The poets used the Japanese tone poem haiku to appreciate the syllabic content of words. Use of the haiku taught prose writers that brevity and simplicity improved their style."

Compressing and refining thought into seventeen syllables forces the writer to select precisely the words that suit the experience being conveyed. Students often say they chose a particularly apt word, one they wouldn't have thought of otherwise, because they needed a certain number of syllables. In their other writing, prose as well as poetry, students find a noticeable improvement after they have focused their minds on the restricted haiku form.

Henderson tells us in *Haiku in English* that haiku writing teaches one how to recognize "what is (or is not) important in any experience." He continues that haiku also teaches "at least the beginnings of the art of compression." Certainly these are important lessons for anyone, child or adult, who wants to practice creative expression.

Hey!
Let's ring
the spring bell.
Blue rain coming down,
flowers speeding up
from the ground.
Hey
let's ring
the Spring bell!

Wayne

A Loop of Seasons

Summer, fall, winter, spring. The seasons of the year affect what we do, what we eat, how we feel. And they are great subjects for poetry.

Poets have traditionally celebrated all the seasons from their own perspective, their own time. From the Romantics, who felt close to the growing season, close to the earth, we have odes to autumn, commemorating the harvest. Haiku writers, as we have seen in the last chapter, often express a perception of the season of the year in writing about specific natural events.

Contemporary poets, children or adults, can write about the seasons from their own perspective. Whether they live in an urban, suburban, or rural area, in a temperate climate or a seasonal one, people can heighten their powers of perception and creative expression by watching and writing about the seasons.

Who doesn't know the feeling of spring fever, winter doldrums, summer lazies? Who hasn't been inspired and exhilarated by a particularly grand seasonal panorama or a small but significant seasonal indication? Observation of the seasons and response to them inspired all the poems you are about to read.

Watch the natural changes, the signs of the seasons: the first change of color, a new smell, a quickening or slowing of activity. These are the material for poetry.

We begin at the new beginning, spring.

Spring

As a subject for poetry, spring has a good deal going for it. Although the signs of spring may be more dramatic in northern climates, they are visible everywhere in the blooming of eucalyptus or apple trees, of cactus or trillium. The first signs of spring suggest a quickening, a renewal. We see plants and animals that weren't there just a day or two ago. The wind is different now; there are new, wet fragrances, a sense of something happening, of movement. We feel a sense of light, lightness, freedom, perhaps of nostalgia.

Mark was a third grader when he wrote "Spring." He was part of a group of about fifty children from a school I had never visited before. I knew none of the children before me, but we had a task to accomplish together. It was mid-May in northern Minnesota, and we could see that spring was finally a reality. We were going to write about that reality. Since none of the children had creative writing experience, I asked their teachers to stay and to write along with us if they wished. I assured them at the outset that we were more interested in lively written expression than in perfect spelling. This is what was written on Mark's paper:

> Spring flose
> in the sky
> and the spring rain
> jumps to plas to plas
> like the mice.
>
> —MARK, AGE 8

If I had been in doubt about any of the words, I would have asked Mark to explain. But I knew exactly what his poem said and could hold it in my hand and read it aloud to his admiring fellow third graders.

One critic mentioned that "from place to place" would sound better than "to place to place." Mark responded seriously, "I'll think about it." I don't know what he finally did. He and the other children each made a copy of their hour's work for me and a copy for themselves. The one I own is Mark's original draft.

Here are some more spring poems by children in other settings. Katie, like many poets before her, sees spring as a beginning:

> A BEGINNING OF A NEW WORLD
> Spring is like a beginning
> of a new world.
> When the flowers open,
> they open one by one.

They seem like they would last
forever.
Baby birds chirp
on their nests,
while their mother
brings a worm.
The snow melts
so much that the city
looks like Venice!

—KATIE, AGE 11

Susan, the nonreader who earlier in the year insisted rightly that *swaggers* was a word, fell headlong into a poems-must-rhyme trap of her own making and offered this:

Spring is here
and summer is near.
Winter is far,
And we'll sing about a star.

—SUSAN, AGE 10

The class came down hard on Susan's poem. But first they pointed out that she could really write interesting things and quoted her "rain swaggers across the street" poem. Only then did they criticize the singsong rhyme and offer the opinion that " 'And we'll sing about a star' is crazy."

Early in the year, Susan would have lashed out at her critics. Early in the year, she would have said, "Everyone picks on me. They hate me." But now Susan merely picked up her poem and regarded the others serenely. "OK," she said, "rhyming is a big pain anyway. I don't know why I messed with it. None of them good words rhyme." Certainly "none of them good words" like *swagger* do.

Third grader Kai imagined the underground "world of worms" with especially strong words. What makes this whole poem *wiggle* in our minds?

> Spring is flowers
> blooming in the sun.
> Robins listen for their
> dinner sliding by
> in the slimy, wet
> world of worms
>
> —KAI, AGE 8

George was only five when I heard him sing the following little spring chant. It ends with a Minnesota child's logical instructions for helping spring hurry up, in a state where one can feel warm wind, see tulips budding, while there are still patches of stubborn snow everywhere:

> The wind is blowing
> and your tulips
> will be coming up.
> It will be time
> to ride in a wagon.
> When the wind blows again,
> the birds will be out
> in their nestes.
> Where is the spring?
> Spring will come
> if you will turn on
> the outside water faucet
> and squirt the water
> on the snow.

And then you will see
the summer grasses.

—GEORGE, AGE 5

Tulips bloom in this spring haiku, and the metaphor is partly embroidery:

GARDEN
Tulips, ric-rac round
 daisies embroidered center,
  carnation napping.

—SUE M., HIGH SCHOOL

Does "powdered puff" give you a different impression from "powder puff"? Read the next poem and see which you like best.

Yellow fuzzed ball
Atop a plant stem,
White powdered puff,
Blowing in the wind . . .
 Dandelion!

—SHELLY, HIGH SCHOOL

The poems and images on spring you have been reading in this chapter avoid overused phrases and worn-out concepts and, instead, let us hear the many individual voices of children.

Op Art! Pop Art! On wing!
Bursting faith!
Dawn
 of
  Spring!

—SHELLY, HIGH SCHOOL

Children can write spring poems at any time of the year. Have the children think about what happens around them in spring. Think about spring words. Fill your chalkboard or paper with the sights, sounds, and colors of spring. Use the mystery box. Write spring cinquains and haiku. Write spring poems when the winter doldrums strike. But especially write spring poems at the height of the season, when everyone can observe firsthand the wonders of spring.

The last spring poem was written by a high school student who signed it Anonymous.

the
dimpled dew-dawn
   s   l   i   d   e   s
      in on the
new-blown wind
leaking
   t
     h
      i
        n
         l
           y
              down the
                 greenly stalk
               of
spring
while
we
   are burnt by the
     summersoon sun.

And so, spring turns into summer.

Summer

For many of us, summertime is the highlight of all the seasons. We wait for summer, when we will have more time to observe and enjoy the world around us. Colors deepen and flare in summer gardens; the sounds of certain birds and insects have come to mean summer to us. The noise of a screen door slamming, the smell of newly cut grass, the splash of swimmers, the murmur of a distant radio, the feel of bare feet on hot cement—all add up to the lazy, shimmering days of summer.

An artist uses particular colors to paint a summer scene. Look at paintings by the French impressionist Renoir. His paintings seem to exist in sunny, warm gardens or on dreamy June rivers with the very essence of a summer day reflected in the light, the air, the skin of the people he puts into his pictures.

Since an artist uses a piece of canvas as a base and colored paints as a medium, the colors themselves must suggest summer sun, breezes, heat, and flower gardens to us. Writers, too, use color to suggest summer. They use color words that can be seen vividly in the mind's eye.

Think of colors. Which ones would you choose to describe a summer scene? Are some colors warmer than others? Can some colors be downright hot? If you list colors in certain clusters, does their mood and intensity change? Look at the following descriptions and notice how many of the words show us a color. Does the first scene feel warm to you? How would you rewrite it if you wanted to make the reader feel cool?

HEAT
I saw a copper bowl in a copper-color room. In the bowl were some oranges and bananas. Nice ripe ones. A blue

and white canary in a very gold cage—singing melody
that made me hot.
The table that the cage was on had a lot of dandelions
on top.

—MARLENE, AGE 11

Calling her scene "A Hot Pacific Day," Katie wrote the following piece.

The toucan and parrots fly in the melting sun. The gold-
enrod is sagging in the sun's blaze. The tired old tiger
yawns lazily to take a nap, while the flamingo cools his
feet in the water. The wilting poppy is dropping very low.
The whole island is damp and sweaty.

—KATIE, AGE 11

Look at the words again. Katie speaks of tropical animals and
birds: *toucan, parrots, tiger, flamingo.* She uses *melting* to describe the sun, and *blaze* to emphasize its heat. Look at her wonderfully tired words: *sagging* and *wilting.* Katie scarcely needs
to tell us that "the whole island is damp and sweaty." We can almost feel its heat and humidity.

In her description of a pond, entitled "Quiet," Anne uses color
words that we usually think of as cool—*green, blue, silver*—yet
there is the warm, still feeling of a summer evening turning into a
summer night. What words do you think help give this impression?

Pebbles are slimy with age. The pool is like a mirror. You
look and see a greenblue pattern of stone. Everything is
quiet—a sleepy quiet. A little ways off, a tired, droning
bee buzzes. Night shadows fall and the pond turns silver,
and quiet pebbles go to sleep.

—ANNE, AGE 12

What happens if you remove the words "a tired, droning bee buzzes"? Does the air cool? Try it.

All of the following poems, written quickly one afternoon by third graders, were simply a fast exercise in the use of color words and strong, hot verbs. In spite of many sessions stressing the use of interesting beginning words, the children began their poems with "The sun . . ." Generally, as a teacher, I try to encourage more diversified beginnings.

> The sun is a lemon,
> A lemon ball.
> It rolls through
> The blue-white hall.
>
> —HELEN, AGE 8

> The sun is bright with its
> Glitter light.
> It blinds you
> When you look up.
> It's steaming hot
> When the colors are red.
>
> —JERRI, AGE 8

> The sun is the key
> to the world's tulips.
> Sit and daydream and
> look at the sun face to face.
>
> —BRANDON, AGE 10

It is hard to imagine feeling hotter than this poem. The universe seems to be on fire:

Beating—
the sizzling hum of heat
    burns my brow.
As the ashes steadily sink
through the sky—
    I die.

        —NANCY, AGE 16

A dry Micronesian season brings forth this cry for relief from the heat:

O rain, come to earth and wet our
souls, for we have thirsted since your
love has left us with Mother Earth.

        —SULIKAU, AGE 16

Osiaol, also from a Micronesian island, wrote: "It seems that we are living in a desert now. Our land is dried up and the plants are all wilted." And she ends with, "Let me just suck my saliva." Quick, somebody, water!

When my daughter Jane was seven, she imagined a squirrel on a hot day. She wrote, "His fur was like strings because he was sweating." And as a fifth grader, she wrote this summer haiku:

Bees surround the fence.
    Honeysuckle tree in bloom,
        counting the flowers.

        —JANE, AGE 10

On that same day, Jane's friend Alison thought of words to describe the slow movement of a sailboat and came up with one of those images that all poets look for, one that "astonishes and delights":

Sailboat:
Snail-walking
toward the west,
its sides shine
with the sun
on them.

—ALISON, AGE 11

Lori's poem lets us feel a lazy summer Sunday morning when even the trees sleep late!

SUNDAY MORNING
The trees sleep late
The peoples' wall of sleep is breaking.
Out in the open bells ring out.
The chorus pours out with song.

—LORI, AGE 10

Flowers, too, can bring to mind the heat of summer, as they do in this next poem:

ORIENTAL POPPIES
Flaming torches!
They flash and sputter a
consuming fire
on gardens already scorched
and bare.

—CATHY, AGE 16

There is also about summertime a sense of faraway sounds, muted perhaps by the very heat itself, which almost visibly hangs in the air. Perhaps summer seems blurred and slow to us because we ourselves are moving slowly, half-hearing summer sounds, seeing life around us as if it were a silent film in slow motion. In her poem "Picnic," a high school writer describes just such a summer state. Listen to the effect of *glued, dull, cottoned.* . . .

PICNIC (A SHORTENED VERSION)
A ghostly throng glued to
     merry-go-round,
     green picnic table,
     barbecue pit.

Dull crash, cottoned shout,
     everyday,
     holiday bare . . .

Who has heard the sun
     singing quietly . . .
     humming to the hazy tune
     of the animals' stream? . . .

The crack of a dry twig, broken,
     re-echos in the air,
     the sound finished
     by a cloud and a tree.

                 —CLARICE, AGE 16

Write summer poems with your children at any time of the year, especially if you aren't in class during the summer. Use long winter afternoons to imagine what summer would be like, were it ever to come again. Fill your chalkboard or paper with myriad summer words, hot words, colorful words, wet words. And have the children write their own pictures of summer.

Autumn

Descriptions of autumn can easily become trite and shopworn—even more easily than descriptive poems about spring. We are tired of the word *falling*, whether it refers to leaves or snow. There must be other words to tell us how things fall. What are they?

Leaves are colored in the autumn. What color? Red? Like what? What else? Another word for yellow? What does it make you see? How do leaves change their colors? Use these questions and others to find new, unusual words to be used in autumn poems.

What strong verbs show how leaves pile up? How the wind blows? How the air changes?

> Red leaves flutter,
> Yellow ones fall.
> Brown leaves gather,
> All along the wall.
>
> —DEBBIE, AGE 10

Debbie's poem has a fine word in the third line. *Gather*, used in an unusual and accurate description, saves the whole poem.

The fall winds blow in each of the three lines of this haiku:

> Scarlet leaves flying,
>   hither and thither they go,
>   scattering autumn.
>
> —LINDA G., HIGH SCHOOL

The idea that leaves can scatter autumn is a departure from the concept that wind scatters leaves. This departure really makes the poem. The other two lines show movement but in much more conventional language.

This next poem belongs to Leslie M. (You may remember her amazingly good haiku from the haiku chapter.) By the time she wrote this she had learned to handle rhyme like a pro:

AGAINST A WHITENED BIRCH
Against a whitened birch,
A fiery flash of red
swirls in the rushing wind
five feet above my head.

Is it a flaming torch?
Is it a burning fire?
Or is it a branch
of scarlet leaves
falling to the mire?

—LESLIE M., AGE 11

Just look at the sophisticated use of words: *whitened, fiery, flash, swirls, rushing, wind.* This autumn tree is no prosaic birch; it is the burning bush. One can only hope Leslie has continued to write poetry.

Watch out the window
  Eerie wind tarnishes—
    Leaves . . . gold . . . remember.

—SUE M., AGE 15

That is a marvelous idea, the autumn wind *tarnishing* the gold leaves, the leaves that can remember being gold.

In Kelly's magical poem, Indian summer is full of the perfume of apples and the glory of that last warm wind:

Autumn
apple-breathed
me
tickling me
with leaves—
and laughed
color
on an
unsuspecting
world—
feigning
to just
wing sunshine.

—KELLY, HIGH SCHOOL

Winter

Winter in the far north, where all of the poems in this section
were written, is more than a season; it is a six- or seven-month
way of life. As a subject for creative writing, it is without limit.
For myself, I believe if I had to choose one word to write about
for the next lifetime or so, I would choose *snow.*

Winter holds every mood, from the ecstasy of the first snowfall
to the despair of never ending March, and words exist to describe
each mood. Because I taught mainly in California, the winter section in this chapter is thin. However, students and poets from all
parts of the country can write about winter—the seasonal
changes in their particular climate, the snow and ice of northern
climates, the moods connoted by these cold, cold images.

For the northerner, winter can be gray, white, and black—

stark, like an etching. It can be enameled blue sky, blinding snow glare, and cobalt shadows. It can be soft dove gray, with white flakes hypnotically falling and falling. Northern winters have more silences than sounds, more challenges than easy times.

How would you express the temperature, the quality of the winter air? Are there words that mean the same as cold? What are they? Does coldness have a sound? A smell? Does ice have color? What are snow colors? What are snow textures? Can you think of another word for *soft*? For *fluffy*? What kinds of jewels (besides diamonds) can we talk about? Have you ever seen pink snow? When is it pink? If you have never seen snow, what have you seen to describe what you imagine snow to be like? Tell us about the winter sun. What words best describe it on a partly sunny day when the temperature is twenty degrees below zero?

Try answering all of these questions in writing with your young poets. Brainstorm for winter words and write them on the chalkboard. Then write winter poems.

> Snow alphabet
> written with a
> childs
>   footprints.
>
> Trees reach
> their snowy
> antlers
> toward the
> snow-falling
> sky.

Judy, age ten, uses an icy image for the sky on a day when the sun is brilliant and the temperature is thirty below zero: "the blue sky was glazed," she tells us. And Katie describes what it feels like to be caught in a real blizzard:

> There is nothing but snow. My hands are getting so numb they are turning blue. When I think of home, I get colder.
> Now a storm is coming up. Snow is spinning and swirling around me. The snow looks like diamonds dancing in a wonderland of blackness.
>
> —KATIE, AGE 11

In seventeen syllables, winter haiku tells the story of this coldest season:

> Snow hurling at me
>   like a cloud of silver-white,
>   lightly covering.
>
> —LISA M., HIGH SCHOOL

Look at the strong image in the second line of this next poem:

> The icing sleet storm
>   Blew the neighborhood jagged—
>   Bits and pieces flew.
>
> —KAY M., HIGH SCHOOL

Finally, Cathy gives us something to think about:

> Winter is a chain locked on my foot,
> And long after winter has gone,
> Its impression remains.
>
> —CATHY, HIGH SCHOOL

When Dan was in ninth grade the school assignment was "Write a Christmas poem." Dan adored computers about as much as he disliked writing poems, so he decided to program an imaginary computer with Christmas words and then record the result:

Sparkle, holly, merry, golden,
Twinkle, gleaming, crimson, streaming,
Glowing, watchful, starry, waiting,
Hurry, supper, presents, wrapping,
Joy, gay, happy, bouncy,
Crack, smash, tinkle, broken,
Shock, quiet, anger, mad,
Tired, sleepy, drowsy, bed
    Warm,
      snug,
        peace.

—DAN, AGE 14

A most satisfying way to harmonize modern technology with the spirit of the season!

Wind, open your mouth
and let the tornado out.
I hear you howling
screaming at my bones,
Barking in the night,
with skies as black as a bat
        floundering in the dark.
                    Melanie

In All Kinds of Weather

There's no need to say that everyone talks about the weather; we all know that's true. Not only does everyone talk about the weather at hand, but many of us can't seem to go to bed at night without listening to a weather forecast—to find out what kind of a day occurred in places remote from us and to see what weather we can expect in the next twenty-four hours.

As an idea starter for writing, weather is a natural. Children seem to vibrate with imaginative interest in all kinds of weather. All through the year, the weather captures everyone's interest. Violent storms or sunny days are equally compelling subjects. Weather poems can be straightforward descriptive scenes. Or children can write about weather as seen by animals, birds, insects, old people, young people, people in various occupations, in various parts of the world. What action words tell us about today's weather? What color words show us a picture of today?

As you read the poems that follow, imagine for yourself how you could present the same theme in two or three different ways. If you are a teacher, consider printing your next publication of the children's writing solely on the topic of weather and including materials produced from a science unit on weather. It's a way to make science interesting for the nonscientific student who enjoys writing, and to make writing interesting for the student who favors science.

Handle matters of spelling and punctuation in the most relaxed way possible. In the first bubbling out of creative juices, nobody wants to have their ideas red-penciled. Children can correct and polish later when they realize that their writing will be published and that clarity is needed to communicate the poem.

Rain

Is it raining? Rain poems are especially fun to write when there's a storm raging outside or when a steady drizzle keeps everyone inside. But they are equally satisfying to conjure up on a sunny day, especially a hot, sunny day. Whether it's raining or not, start by filling the chalkboard or sheets of paper with rain words.

Every parent knows that a rainy day at home cries out for "something to do." "Rain-storming" can bring you some real gifts!

Set out the paper, pencils, and some colorful markers for the art that will illustrate the poems, and see what happens.

Now's the time to think of wet words and stormy words. Conjure up the names of things that can hang down like the streams of rain when there is no wind. What words come to mind? I've done this with my students and listened as they called out words like "threads" and "strings." What do we do with thread or string? Can rain weave, or tie, or knot? What can happen in your poem if you use these word pictures?

Spattering raindrops reminded third grader Shelly of something unusual:

> Rain comes gushing
> down like confetti.
> I like the rainbow
> that comes when
> the rain and the sun are
> mixed together.
>
> —SHELLY, AGE 8

Rainbows come into the heads of young poets when we talk about the rain.

Billy called his poem "To the Wind," and he imagined a wonderfully different rainbow:

> Loosen the knot of birds.
> Don't ruffle the leaves.
> Don't rattle the trees.
> Don't blow over the
> bikes. Fold the rainbow
> neatly.
>
> —BILLY, AGE 9

And Sheri gives us a surprise in this poem. There are images here that we will not forget!

> Old rooftops twitch
> in the rain.
> Then, like magic
> everything stands
> still. The only sound
> is the coughing of the house.
> It stretches out to read the
> weather
> and falls asleep.
>
> —SHERI, AGE 9

Let's talk about the sounds of rain. Ask the children what they hear on a rainy day. If someone obliges by bringing up *pitter patter*, explain that this is an overworked expression. If rain really sounds like *pitter patter*, what else does it sound like?

Terry has her own variation on that overworked sound of rain. Her rain goes "plitter platter." Albert writes that the rain on his roof says "toc—toc—toc."

Let your ears hear noises only a rain-slicked day can bring. Do you hear cars going by? What special sound do the cars' tires make on wet pavement? Is there a strong word for that sound? Can that sound be compared to something else? In the following poem a third grader succinctly describes the sound car tires make:

> When the cars
> Run over the rain,
> It slaps the sidewalk.
>
> —JOE, AGE 8

His twin brother, Tom, said it this way:

> When it rains
> It storms and pours
> And the cars going by
> Seem like their tires
> Are split in two
> By rain.

—Tom, AGE 8

". . . tires . . . split in two by rain" really lets us hear the ripping sound of tires on a wet street.

When eliciting responses about the sound of rain from children, we can ask, "Is there any musical instrument you think of when you imagine rainy noises?" Wolfram heard a small, tinkling instrument and wrote this poem:

> When the rain came down
> In the dark day
> It came down
> Like little bells tinkling.
> It clattered like little rocks.

—Wolfram, AGE 10

Beverly thought of thunder as a drum. She had a fine first line one day, but she couldn't get anywhere with it. So we put it on the chalkboard for the third grade to share. "The drumbeat of thunder" was now everybody's possible first line. After an afternoon of intermittent interest in that one line, Barry wrote a second line that the class approved of. We added his line to Beverly's:

> The drumbeat of thunder
> Is pounding away

Interest was immediately revived. Everyone began looking for a third line. When Robert offered his suggestion, "on the dead white steeples," the debate was hot and furious. Most of the class felt that "dead steeples" were "too spooky." (Their teacher thought privately that it was a wonderfully strange image!) Reluctantly, Robert changed the image to "high steeples" and then added another line to end the poem. Here is the finished poem:

> The drumbeat of thunder
> Is pounding away
> On the high, white steeples
> Over the bay.

I've included this example of another kind of group effort to illustrate the ongoing interest which can be generated in a classroom where the opportunity to work and play with words is constant and where an individual's efforts at expression are regarded seriously by student and teacher alike.

Suppose rain is a person. Can you imagine this rain? How does it move? Where does it go? What is rain wearing? Susan personified rain in the poem you already read in the introduction:

> Rain swaggers across the street
> Rain skips across the alleys
>   of the world . . .

—SUSAN, AGE 10

Here is another way of seeing the rain as a person:

> Every time
> When it is raining hard
> and you are in your house
> and the rain splashes on your roof,

It sounds like a man is on your roof,
and it sounds like he is hammering a nail
on top of your roof.

—PEGGY B., AGE 9

What do you see on a rainy day? Are there colors in the rain? What colors can you see? Are there colorful wet things that show up in the rain? What are they?

Ann made up the following rainy day word picture:

The colors of rain
Are like a rainbow in the sky.
The cars have a SWASH as they go by.
The people in their yellow raincoats go by.
As they walk
A wiggly shadow is behind them.
The rain on the rooftop
goes pitter patter
all day long.

—ANN, AGE 8

The triteness of the phrase "pitter patter" is more than offset in this poem by the other language. Not only can we see the people in their "yellow raincoats," but we can also see their "wiggly shadows" distorted by the rain.

Suppose rain had a hardness to it, like gemstones. What would hard rain be like? The word *diamonds* occurred to one of the third graders I was working with. After taking its place on our chalkboard, it appeared in several poems. Here is one of them:

One day the rainbow
Slashed across the sky

With a gold, silver, and copper sparkle.
It looked like little diamonds.

—CORINNE, AGE 8

Notice the strong word *slashed* in this poem; it allows us to see the knife-edged rainbow Corinne saw in her imagination.

And Susan, age ten, says that the rain "twinkles and sprinkles crystally in the sky like diamonds on a bride." Susan made her comparison of rain to diamonds especially effective by her twin verbs "twinkles and sprinkles" and her invented adverb *crystally*.

Here is a rain poem with a little different kind of hardness to it:

Crystal wires of rain
Capture me
then shatter. Freedom!

—ANN N., HIGH SCHOOL

How does rain move? Ask the students for some good, lively words for the way rain moves along the street, over puddles, against windows, through trees. The word *skips* appeared on our chalkboard. It appealed to Susan, Richard, and to other children as well. Here is Richard's poem:

Thunder walks
through the rain
and lightning skips
lightly by.

—RICHARD, AGE 9

Thunder takes its time. We can hear it walking through the rain. And the "lightning skips lightly by" faster than thunder and not nearly so noisily. These are extremely apt images.

See the animals in the wet outdoors. See their fur, their ears, their reflections in streets, puddles, windows. How do animals feel about rain? Do cats and ducks have the same feeling about rain? Imagine you are an animal in the rain. If you were an animal, how would the rain make you feel?

Think about plants. See the rain on petals, dripping off leaves, bending stems. Is there a special smell the wet earth gives off? Can you find words for that damp, mossy fragrance? Nancy wrote a haiku to describe the aftermath of a spring shower:

Each wet tulip cup
　Tosses its head, pouring out
　　Cloud-pitchers of rain.

　　　　　　　　　　　　　—NANCY W., AGE 14

Think about puddles. Can you see children and puddles? Look hard at those children as they run through the puddles. What do children running through the puddles sound like? Think of some strong action words to describe a child's feet meeting a puddle.

Think about puddles and rain, with no children in sight. Does this poem let you see a puddle in a new way?

When the raindrops fall
on a puddle,
They look like shooting-stars
In the blue mud-puddle sky.

　　　　　　　　　　　　　—ELVIRA, AGE 10

This has the fresh sound and impact of real poetry. I don't believe I've ever read "blue mud-puddle sky" before. Have you?

Wind

An invisible force, the wind has always stirred imaginations of writers. The push and shove of moving air is a theme with endless variations. No matter where we live, wind is a common experience.

> I see the wind
> black and icy
> coming toward me
> with
> beating fists
> against
>   my
>   face. —julie

So ask your children, "What does the wind do?" The word that comes to everyone's mind is *blow!* And it goes up there on the chalkboard or paper to begin the torrent of wind words that will appear as the students start to think. But what else means blow? Think of a word that means to blow very hard. Someone says *rage;* another suggests *sweep;* still another offers *rushes.* These are good words that go on the chalkboard to join the others. Following are three poems that use the word *rushes:*

The wind
Rushes your kite
and tears your kite
and pushes your kite!

—ROGER, AGE 8

The wind rushes to the sun
And takes his place.

—GAYNELL, AGE 8

The wind rushes across
the green meadows.
It blows my hair
Like purple thistles
In the sky.
It blows my dress and petticoat
like dry leaves
Sailing high.

—ELVIRA, AGE 10

Jerry lets us hear all sorts of wind noises in this picture of kites:

Kites are in the air.
When the wind blows against the kites
It cracks the kites.
And it tears and rips the kites
to pieces.
Winds blow as hard as a fan.
The wind whistles and roars as loud
as thunder.

—JERRY, AGE 8

Look at those snapping, strong words—*cracks, tears, rips*—and
see what they do for the poem. They are all short, striking words
with hard consonant sounds. This is not a gentle wind.

In this next poem the wind is also tearing:

> When the kites are in the air
> it seems like the wind stops the kites
> from flying.
> When the wind blows
> it looks like the wind
> tears the leaves
> off the trees!
>
> —JOE C., AGE 9

Is there color in the invisible wind? Young poets say there is
indeed:

> There is a silver wind
> It would push you down
> Orange wind at sunset,
> Because it's so nice,
> That's why.
>
> —JERRY, AGE 8

Beverly sees the wind as both a color and a shape:

> The wind is a copper shape
> And it rolls and rolls
> Till it is a bowl.
>
> —BEVERLY, AGE 9

Think about the smell of wind. What does it depend upon?
Can we guess where the wind has been by breathing it?

If you went by a bakery
When the wind was blowing,
The wind would smell like
Baker's hot bread,
Hot buns,
Hot cakes.

—JERRY P., AGE 8

The following poem originated in a seacoast town in northern California:

I went outside with my kite
And the wind smelled
Like salt
That came from the sky.

—AUDREY, AGE 10

Kim used the idea of saltiness, too, but in a different way:

The kite glides across the sky
with a swishing noise.
The sky is full of
many fish.
The fish fly across
The salty sky.

—KIM, AGE 8

Now stretch your mind again. Think of the wind as a person. Who is this windy fellow? Or is it a woman you see blowing about? What does the wind wear? How old is the wind? What does wind do? What does it use? Emily Dickinson wrote that "the wind tapped like a tired man," and Carl Sandburg spoke of a spendthrift wind that walked through an apple orchard "counting his money and throwing it away."

How do you see the wind: strong? kind? mean? The following poems show how some children personified the wind:

The trees bow low
When the wind rides by,
Because they know
He's King of the Sky.

—VICKIE, AGE 8

Vickie's wind has a dash of grandeur about him.

The wind is like an old man
and he blows softly
Over the sun.

—RONNIE, AGE 9

Here is a teasing wind:

Oh, oh! My hat!
The wind has stolen
My hat!
I can't get it.
Now I have it,
And the wind laughs at me.
That was a big joke!

—MARGO, AGE 9

In the following bit of prose, called "The Ages of Wind," the wind is also personified:

The wind sweeps across the earth like a poised young princess, thrashes itself against cold brownstone buildings, spins like a used top, and ends like an old woman staggering on the top of a hill.

—MARY S., AGE 12

And Anne L., age ten, wrote, "The fingers of Wind are curling around defenseless trees."

This next poem has a misty feeling that is lovely, and the last line is an unusual description of birds:

It is a windy night and
    a stormy night
and the dusk is all around,
In the air,
and on the northern
    plains of Minnesota.

High in the air, the wind is rough
and the fog is the mist of
    the hills.
The birds fly around in the air
Trying in vain
To find their homes,
With their wings of rain
and their bodies of wetness.

—JANE, AGE 10

Every once in a while, a poem "wants to rhyme" and we let it. Emily had a tendency, at age eight or nine, to think in rhyme, but her poems often avoided that deadly "moon-spoon-June" writing of children. Her awareness of the power of words is revealed in the following poem:

THE WIND
The wind is quite a lively thing,
Carrying tunes that bluebirds sing,
Howling, whistling, soaring away
Off to the shores of the sparkling bay.
When he gets angry,
Waters splash.
As he begins to fight and lash,
Leaves go flying through the air,
Crackling, swishing
Here and there!

—EMILY, AGE 9

Emily uses *soaring* and *lash* like an old pro—and with excellent results.

Here then, you have the wind, as seen by children. Constant searching for the right word, the new comparison, the fresh image will help you and your students create a sweeping windstorm in your classroom too. We expect it to blow away the cobwebbed phrases and mildewed, overworked ideas forever!

Third-Grade Weather Myths

During a unit on weather, California third graders grew most knowledgeable about the water cycle; the reasons for snow formations and rainfall; the theories behind light refraction and rainbows. Along with their scientific probings, they read many myths and legends from ancient peoples who also sought to explain these same phenomena.

Quite naturally, the children began inventing their own tales to explain to their "people" the frightening and mysterious natural happenings around them. The following prose selections are some of the *Stories of Magic Reasons* that resulted from their interest in science and their delight in writing:

THE LEGEND OF THE STAMPING HORSE

Once, many, many years ago, there lived a horse. No one could catch the horse because it was the horse of lightning. Every time men tried to catch the horse it ran so fast that it made lightning!

Then one day the horse was caught. Famous horse trainers came and they found out that this horse was the stamping horse of lightning.

The men called to the men at the stall, "Open the gate." And they opened the gate and suddenly the sky blackened and lightning roared.

And then ALL the men knew that this running horse was the horse of lightning.

—ROGER, AGE 9

The sky is strange. The snow crystals have six points on them. The lightning devil is very mean. He only comes out when it is stormy. His horns are very hot and red and his tail is sharp as an arrow and his body is like fire. He is red all over except his eyes: they are YELLOW and RED!

—MIKE, AGE 8

LIGHTNING AND THUNDER

Once a man had some lightning in one of his hands and thunder in his other hand. His name was Adad and this was long ago. He was angry all the time. He was not a good man at all. He would throw his thunder around. The people did not like him at all. He had long hair too. It was very long. When he goes by people, he throws his thunder.

—LEANNE, AGE 8

THE BUFFALO HERD

Once upon a time some Indians were going hunting. They saw some buffalo. The Indians began to chase the buffalo. When the Indians shot a buffalo, lightning came out of their horns. So every time you see lightning you will know why.

When the buffalo fell it thundered. When they ran it thundered too.

—CHRIS, AGE 9

THE WIND

Once upon a time there was a man who told fairy tales about the wind. He said that the wind was a witch sweeping her floor with her broom in the air. That made the wind blow real hard and her hands can make wind go fast and make trees go back and forth. And she can make it stop too. The wind is dangerous because it can make a tidal wave in the ocean. You cannot see the wind but it can feel you all the time.

—JOHN, AGE 8

THE SNOW AND ITS MAGIC

Once upon a time there was a train. And it carried horses high in the sky. But these are secret horses. Do you know what they do? When they throw back their

manes the jewels flutter down to earth. So that is why
there is snow.

—KIM, AGE 8

RAIN
Rain came in with the
fog.
Rain came down
like needles
sewing thick
cloth.
Fog came down
like a veil.

—DAVID, AGE 8

What causes the weather? Ask your children!

Frost-bitten trees
Snapping in the cold air.
Icicles like Diamond
Knives
Fall with a
<u>Piano-splintered</u> sound.

Mrs. Ellerbroch's sixth grade

Stretching
my strong steel bones
across the red river,
I'm not going to last too long...
farewell.

Jolene, age 11

City

Today's urban community presents a rich source of ideas for writing. Except for those written by the young Micronesians, the poems in this book have all been written by city children and teens; but the poems included in the book thus far have mostly reflected their feelings about nature and natural phenomena rather than their interest in the city for its own sake.

Now let's turn to the city itself, in all its complexity and variety. The possibilities for poem ideas, as we've said before, are always endless, no matter where we choose to look. The city is no exception. A quick listing of some city subjects may be helpful here.

buildings	signs and posters
noises	textures
people	building demolition
animals	construction
movement	clocks
color	steeples
lights	store windows
sun and shadow	trash cans
rain and reflections	theater marquees
snow	wires
rooftops	poles
alleys	elegance
litter	poverty
fire escapes	vehicles
personal feelings	parks
tenements	escalators
elevators	

Whether your children are city dwellers or only visit the city now and then, you will no doubt add many ideas to this bare beginning. Each item on this list can, and should, suggest further images for the writer to use. Children will think of topics themselves. Encourage them to write about the parts of the city they know best. What does their neighborhood look like? Do they live in apartment buildings, houses, in the suburbs, in the city itself? Do they walk to school or take a bus? How do they see their city?

Sherry sees the city in summer. She enjoys playing with opposites in her poem:

> Water, ice,
> cool ponds and lakes,
> blue-green water falling.
> You are starving for this
> on a hot city night.
>
> —SHERRY Z., AGE 13

The long, hot, muggy days seem one hundred times worse to city dwellers who must live with streets, sidewalks, and sides of buildings reflecting the heat. Instead of telling us about the hot searing sun on metal and concrete, Sherry focuses on something quite different. The result is a poem about city heat that uses only cool words.

Ben's city is smog bound, and his choice of words here is particularly effective:

> Windows and buildings crusted
> with sediment of progress
> choking the senses with a fatal
> wind-blown cloud.
>
> —BEN W., AGE 15

Crusted lets us know that the dirty layers of smoke have been piling up on the windows and buildings for a long time. He uses *sediment* for the same reason. It is a word often used to describe the slow sifting of powdered rock through water. And his ironic use of *progress* is a strong choice. *Choking* and "fatal wind-blown cloud" tell it all, dramatically.

Many of the poems in this chapter were created one morning in Minneapolis by students I was meeting for the first time. The mystery box idea lends itself particularly well to the city topic, so after we talked about writing, about playing with words, and after we put many city words on the chalkboard, each of the children picked a topic from the mystery box.

You can start with the city at a particular time of day. Can you see the city at night? Its lights move or run or blink or stare, depending on your point of view. What does night hide? What do lights illuminate? How does the city by night differ from the city by day?

Carolyn places her dirty city under early morning light, before things begin their mad move and dash. Perhaps the factories are still asleep, too, for she lets us smell air that is "like fields of grass":

Dim lights
shine on the city.
Early morning
is
a magenta morning
and a gold copper morning.
Air is like fields
of grass.

—CAROLYN, AGE 8

Look at a single building. What does it look like during the day? What does the same building look like at night?

Think about alleys. Think about corners. Think about tall buildings that block out the sky. What are the special feelings city people have when they see themselves closed in on all sides by hard, high walls? Can you describe these city feelings?

Or think of an old, old building about to be demolished. Look, with your mind, at the scroll shapes, the fancy carving, the points and tower shapes. What has this graceful old relic seen? Can you

see the new city through the eyes of an old building about to die
at the hands of the demolishing crew?

What shapes do we find in city shadows—lines? grids? Are
there triangles of shadow? What can cast a round shadow? an
oval one? a zigzag shadow? When the sun is at high noon, what
happens to the shadows of buildings, of people? When the sun
is low in the sky, how do shadows change? Do shadows have
color?

Who could name all the things there are to look at in the city?
One great place to look at almost anything and everything is store
windows. And Roberta's focus in this poem is on the doll-like
mannequins that show off clothes:

Posing—
Alive or dead?
Modeling all day long
Standing stiff, staring at people
all day.

—ROBERTA, AGE 12

Not a real person here, either, but a bridge personified speaks
the sad, lonely lines in Jolene's quiet cinquain:

Stretching
my strong steel bones
across the red river,
I'm not going to last too long . . .
farewell.

—JOLENE, AGE 11

Here is another poem about a bridge with a very different mood.

RIVERS, BOATS AND BRIDGES
Glimmering nights over the river
are very glamorous.
Boats with their lights look like
cakes with candles and bridges
look like ribbons.

—ANNA L., AGE 9

Think about city animals. Where are we to look for them? The city has them, of course. Think about birds. Which ones fly free in the city? Which birds live in cages? There are dogs and there are cats—elegant, pampered ones and ragged, neglected ones.

Can you imagine a poem about rats? Cockroaches? What are some rat words? Think of cockroach words. How do rat words differ from words that make us see and feel the *insectness* of a cockroach? Is there a difference in the weight of the words? The way they move? Describe a rat's leg. Now describe a cockroach's leg. Words can let us see each kind of leg. Try it!

Imagine an anthill on a busy city street. How are the people rushing by like the ants scurrying about the anthill? What do people look like to ants?

Some of the city's wild animals live in zoos. "City Tiger" is the title of the next poem.

I
roar
and have many stripes.
I eat steak every day.
I live in a small cement cage
—and dream.

—DEJOHN G., AGE 12

The writer said he wanted to contrast the good (steak every day) with the bad (the small cage) from the tiger's point of view; and he wanted to let us know that the tiger wishes for his own jungle home. Do you think he's achieved this? Look at the last two words. All the longings for freedom a tiger could possibly feel are summed up by "—and dream."

Nora's mystery box topic was "the zoo." She had a strange idea of who lives at the zoo—and some feelings about being caged:

THE ZOO
The zoo is where some
animals stay every night and day.
But there seems to be a little
girl in a cage too.
My, my!
Is this the zoo?

—NORA W., AGE 9

And what about people in the city? We have a whole chapter in this book devoted to people of all kinds. When we concentrate on city people specifically, do we find some traits or attitudes that seem different from country people or people in small towns?

Even though airplanes are air-conditioned, travel is tiring, and Ann has seen the people boarding planes at a big city airport in summer. What do the words "paper people" and "cutout humans" make you see? Are the words well chosen?

Airplane.
Sun's rays on wings—
Paper people wilting,
cutout humans are not caring
in flight.

—ANN W., AGE 13

Seeing the city as a lonely place, Mary Beth draws us this picture of a man whose aloneness is a symbol of the impersonal city:

The brick walls . . . with brick upon brick
following the wall,
the gray slabs
cracked with age,
old and worn.

The tops meet the gray skies
filled with swiftly fleeting clouds
as,
cold and uninviting,
the roofs of the city loom:
patches of cement fields
broken by soaring be-speckled
pigeons.
A man walks—the gray slabs
unaware—
The cement fields . . .
         . . . the brick walls.

—MARY BETH, HIGH SCHOOL

The people in Tim's elevator poem seem to echo the impersonal tone of the preceding poem. We get a sense of weariness
and separateness from the words "heads are hanging" and from
the description of the people as they "slip off into the crowd." The
poem suggested itself to Tim when he chose a new kind of mystery slip in addition to the one giving him a subject idea, *elevator*.

On this new slip was written a word that the writer must use
as the first word in a poem. *Solemn* was the word that sparked
Tim's mind that afternoon with the following result:

Solemn people on an elevator:
Heads are hanging
people are staring at the floor.
When the first floor comes,
they slip off into the crowd.

      —TIM, AGE 10

Seth saw this city scene:

Mourning
a love gone by
he lives on a park bench.
A mansion floats into
his dream at night.

                         —SETH, AGE 11

CITY BIRDS
Flights of birds weave
their wings
on a loom
of windows!

—STEPHANIE, AGE 11

If we think about the way city people move, what words come to mind? There are people on sidewalks, people in stores, in elevators, on the street, in restaurants—how do they act?

"Speedy," the sixth graders said. They *dash, push, shove, rush, run, crowd, pull, yank, jab.* Debbie imagined the Christmas rush when she wrote:

Shoving, crowded shoppers
do not
have fun
when they are in a hurry.
Christmas shopping.

—DEBBIE, AGE 12

At a fire, people act in certain ways, and a sixth grader tells us about them:

Red truck,
blowing siren,
people screaming, yelling!
Water spraying, people saying
Fire! Fire!

—D. M., AGE 12

And Joan's "Supermarket" is a frenzied place indeed:

Wide,
    big—
baskets of groceries
    and carts speeding
faster, faster—
    people run to clerk—
        zooming carts.

—JOAN, AGE 11

But all descriptions of city people do not need to be pictures of frantic or noisy individuals. The city shows us its quiet moods, too, and sounds become dulled sometimes, dull enough, perhaps, to let us hear birds call:

ALONE IN THE DARK
I was sitting on the front porch
and I could feel
the slick and silky wind
whirl
about my shivering arms . . .
and I felt the gloomy night
coming
and the crows cawing.

—MARY B., AGE 10

There is a fine sense of approaching dark in that little poem.

When we consider the essence of the city, we certainly think of its sounds. "Deafening noise" was the first reaction of a group of sixth graders in an inner-city school to the question "What do you hear in the city?" The chalkboard soon resounded with *rumble, pounding, clank, scraping, clang, boom, roar, squeal, thump, squeak, sonic boom, smash, clash, crash.*

Tell about sirens, I suggested. The words came: *screaming, wailing, yelling,* a *howl,* a *red shriek,* a *white scream.*

What makes the big noises? The empty spaces on their own paper and on the chalkboard filled up: *jets, trucks, bulldozers, wrecking ball, sirens, ambulances, whistles, bells, cars, buses, helicopters, motorbikes, parade, street sweeper, police cars.* If you read the list aloud, you'll hear it fairly roar at you.

Every imaginable kind of motorized vehicle rumbles and sputters along city streets. In the chapter "Animating the Inanimate," we find trucks compared to ants or elephants. In the poem "Cars at Night" in that same chapter, they are animals, "released from their cages . . . blinking their eyes."

Bill's cement mixer menaces us:

GIANT
. . . thundering—
crunching rock, gravel, and sand,
it moves.

—BILL, AGE 11

The words "it moves" evoke a ponderous, sinister, unstoppable thing. *Thundering, crunching,* and *moves* are heavy sounds. If Bill had said *bites* instead of *crunching,* the whole poem would be lighter and quicker. Or, if he had said the machine was being driven instead of saying it *moves,* we would have lost the whole feeling of the cement mixer being ominously alive, moving by itself. Try it and see for yourself.

The machines don't move on their own, though. This next poem reminds us that people move machines, and not always wisely:

THE SEMI CRASH
Move, move!
That's what he says.
But you don't listen. Pow!
Boxes flying, cans upsetting,
crack up!

—SHERRY Z., AGE 13

You and the children can focus on a multitude of city images. Eric and Sherry write about garbage and trash with words that let us see, hear, and almost smell what they are picturing. This is a great subject to play with at home, of course!

Shattering the morning,
the garbage man
is clanging the cans.
My ears will be ringing
'till I'm half deaf
before the sun comes up.

—ERIC W., AGE 10

Sherry's plastic trash bags seem to have gone mad. Can you imagine the sky full of exploding bags?

Bursting
egg shells, potato skins
over the street,
garbage bags explode
into the sky.

—SHERRY Z., AGE 13

"City wind" was the subject of the following poems. As the children called out their windiest words, the chalkboard began to give back poem ideas. We wrote words that mean *blow* but are fiercer: *rip, tear, shove, flatten, whip, stirs up, twisting, stings, burns.*

We spoke of city things that are moved by wind—dust, fragments of glass, papers, candy wrappers—and tried to come up with words to describe smoke in some new ways. Eric looked at our chalkboard full of wind words and added one of his own, *spores,* to describe smoke particles. The following excellent word picture is the result:

A frozen wind blows 'cross the town.
It flattens buildings and stirs up dust.
A harsh northwind blows spores of smoke
and it spreads and crinkles like papers
     on the street.

—ERIC W., AGE 10

Tim looks at the city through the imaginary eyes of the wind:

Broken glass in the alley,
Broken glass in the street.
I am the city wind.
I whip through slums
On a rainy day.

—TIM, AGE 10

Nora wanted to write about the wind, too, and for her first word drew a slip of paper with *frantic* printed on it. I find this to be an effective way to solve the "how shall I begin . . ." problem. And it sometimes serves to introduce some new words to younger children. Nora didn't know what *frantic* meant. She could have exchanged it for another word. But after she got a sense of its meaning, she decided it was a good word for a wind poem and that she would try to use it. Here is her result:

Frantic wind
sounds like rock and roll bands,
like doors slamming.
And blowing wind
sounds like whistles,
in the bands.

—NORA, AGE 9

Bursting was the word Sarah picked as her first word. There is a great deal happening in her poem: "papers fly through the air," they are "bursting through the city."

Bursting papers fly through the air,
Bursting through the city in a flash!
The wind rises up and down as it blows
from street to street.

—SARAH, AGE 7

Action words fill this next poem, too:

Twisting and twirling,
Jumping and throwing,
It stings, it burns,
It blows!
It is the city wind!

—ANNA L., AGE 9

Sarah, a second grader, picked a subject slip labeled *fire escapes* and a first-word slip, *muttering*. She decided to use them together, and the sudden image "muttering fire escapes" gave her imagination a whole scenario to share with us in this delightful poem:

Muttering fire escapes
pass secrets through the night.
They whisper to the wind
and the wind talks back
with a
swish
swish
swish.

—SARAH, AGE 7

Have we seen the city as a diverse source for writers? It has many faces, many sides, endless idea possibilities. We have only scratched the surface here. Expand the suggestions I've offered. Be specific if you like. Name the building you are describing. Tell us who, exactly, the person is you are writing about. Let us know your city in a particular mood or time of day. City children can tap these rich possibilities for a long time to come.

This morning i saw
blue caterpiler mending
a rusty old wet leaf
that fel in the breeze

Morning

What does the word *morning* bring to mind? Say the word; think about it: morning . . . morning . . . morning. What do you see? Think about the earliest, faintest beginnings of morning—in spring, summer, autumn, winter. How does daybreak change from season to season?

What are the colors of morning? How do the colors of night change as light comes to the sky, to the land, to the water? What color words show us a winter morning? a hot summer morning? What colors are in a rainy morning?

Let your mind's eye see morning light in the country, at the sea's edge, in the city. Think about shadow and sunlight. See corners, angles, spires, fire escapes, trucks, cars, telephone poles. See the shadows they cast in the morning sun.

What are morning's smells? Are they heavy or light? Salt breeze? Newly mown hay? Breakfast cooking?

How does morning make you feel? Do you get up early to greet the sun? Or do you bury your head under the covers? What are some words that describe how you feel in the morning?

What are the sounds of early morning, the ones you hear before you're even awake? Early birds? The garbage collector rattling cans in the alley? An alarm clock that won't shut up? Someone calling you to breakfast?

What are the sounds of a morning in winter? In the north, the sound of flocks of birds at their dawn feeding is conspicuously missing. What are some sounds that are missing from your winter morning? What do you hear instead? Now put the missing sounds into a spring morning. What does your inner ear hear?

Children have no trouble at all letting their minds respond to these exploring questions. Ask them. As you focus in more and more sharply on imaginative visions of morning, your paper will fill up with suggestions, images, sound words, color words, and comparisons.

Compare morning to something else. Is it a man? A woman? An old person? A child? Is it an animal, a bird, or an insect? What kind of machine could bring us morning? Does a creature bring us morning? Does the persona of morning change with the seasons?

In the poem "Fern Hill," Dylan Thomas called morning a "wanderer white," a young man, striding the hills with a rooster on his

> ## Morning
>
> You lie in bed
>   all is silent.
> Suddenly night leaves
>   And light takes its place
> Shining like a ball of fire
>   Like a parade
> cymbals!
> horns!
> drums!
> You know then
>   Morning has arrived.
>
>   By Kim

shoulder. Do you think of morning as a strong young man? How do you see him? Why do you think he is wandering instead of sitting on a hill? If you were morning, would you choose a rooster as your companion?

In Kathy's poem we see the sun as a hearty, jovial sort of morning-bringer:

Fresh white clouds gather
Together in wordless company
To meet the rising sun,
Then quickly scatter
Before its boisterous greetings.

—KATHY, HIGH SCHOOL

The next two poems compare morning with animals. In the first, we are not told what the animal is. Have you an idea?

First it comes, wild with fury
and delight. It is mad to be
held in captivity and happy
to be out. It is so happy that
it wants to stay on and on. But
the night won't let it; so after
awhile day begins to fade away.

—JANET S., AGE 11

In this next poem, a most unusual animal is compared to morning:

MORNING'S GLORY
I woke up one glorious day
To see a wonderful sight
Before my eyes
Like a leaping frog
The morning impatiently
    Excitedly
Pushed away Mr. Night.

—JEAN H., AGE 10

When Pat's "midnight birds" in this next poem turned out to be roosters, the class wondered. But she firmly left the phrase in her poem. Read it and see what you think about the "midnight birds":

Midnight birds crowed their morning call.
Bubbles dewed the earth.

Dancers rainbowed my garden—
... the sun burst darkness ...

—PAT, HIGH SCHOOL

Predawn dark, the pale, early light, and day's full burst of sun
all figure in the following poems about morning and daybreak:

Cold and still ... golden sun rays
blooming out against the everlasting dark
blue sky ... light ... extreme brightness.

—FABYAN, AGE 20

Kim's poem thrusts us suddenly and loudly into morning:

You lie in bed
    all is silent.
Suddenly night leaves
    And light takes its place
Shining like a ball of fire
    Like a parade
    cymbals!
    horns!
    drums!
You know then
    Morning has arrived.

—KIM, AGE 11

Another parade image lets us hear the vibrant noises of day:

GAIETY IN THE MORNING
Morning is here!
Like coronets, snare drums

Tooting and pounding
Noisily bringing midday near.

—JEAN H., AGE 10

The notion of morning as a collection of bright sounds appealed to several of the children. A brass band was a favorite image to play with:

MORNING
Morning comes like a big
parade with the brass
colored sun at the head.
The misty wind is blowing
with a gay and jolly sound.

—MARY R., AGE 10

The image of the "brass colored sun" is a good one. We can see and hear the brass section of the band at the head of the parade. Might this poem have been stronger if other sections of the band had followed? What instrument makes a sound like "the misty wind"? What other instruments might play in morning's parade?

In one class we explored a number of sun shapes. What is the sun anyway, besides round and yellow? Is it ever pink or green or any other color? Is it ever not round? What else is round like the sun?

Two eight-year-olds plucked the word *doorknob* from the list of sun shapes on the chalkboard. However, the word evoked two very different images:

Daisy doorknob!
The sun
looks

as if it is
two inches
away.

—KEVIN M., AGE 8

MORNINGRISE
Mmmmmm—smell the flowers—
rust rose, violet blue.
Rusty rose
is a good smell
and the sun is a yellow
that no one's ever seen.
It is like a doorknob
in the sky.
I wonder—
if I opened it,
would it turn
to night?

—BECKY H., AGE 8

Think of the image that must have come into eight-year-old Kai's head when he described the way the sun pours through his front door! Those "cartwheels of light" are unforgettable.

The sun glows brilliantly
throwing
cartwheels of light
through our front door
and
robins sing with charms
of laughter
on a summer day.

Think about the phrase "charms of laughter," too. There is a marvelous sense of delight and joy in these words!

The sun's rays themselves become solid, stemlike in this next cinquain:

Golden,
amber rods poke
stems of spiraling light
underneath the blue grasses
of sky.

—NANCY W., AGE 14

Nancy wrote a haiku, too, to describe an early spring morning after a shower:

Each wet tulip cup
   Tosses its head, pouring out
      Cloud-pitchers of rain.

—NANCY W., AGE 14

Have you ever known the frustration of oversleeping? In the following poem, Janet shows us the frustration of racing from nighttime to morning's finish line—and losing:

YOU DREAM
You dream about it all night,
dream that you will wake up
with it. Only somehow no matter
how hard you think, hope and
dream about it, it always
beats you. Day is not a
sleepy head.

—JANET S., AGE 11

There are sleepy, dim words at the beginning of this next poem, and then as day comes, the words begin to grow hard and bright and to move rapidly until the last line:

Blackness softer than rain
Blanketed the drowsy world
And guarded it with dimly
    shining stars.
Cold sunrise
Drowned the sleeping darkness,
Flooding the unsuspecting earth
with hard, unyielding light.
Crickets scurried from
    the harsh day
To the shelter of
    cement cracks
    and rock piles
And awaited the evening.

                  —KATHY, HIGH SCHOOL

Of all the young people I've known, Kelly was one of the most inventive in her use of words. She used nouns as verbs—*lemoned*; nouns as adverbs—*sunly*; and, in general, romped and played with the language as though she owned it.

Morning
sunly
lemoned its way
in today,
cheered on
by birds—
applauded
and kissed

by daisies—
leaving only
yellowed footprints
for afternoon
to guess.

—KELLY, HIGH SCHOOL

When Susan found an empty eggshell one morning in Wales, she wrote this poem and brought it to us, her American family, as a gift. Look at all the words she has used to show hollowness, emptiness: *nullity, cave, parting, blankness, silence, empty*. The entire poem gives an atmosphere of stillness and peace:

Awake.
See the pale blue of a morning sky,
a nullity, a purity.
A bird's egg,
shell empty,
fallen bare
to lie among dying flowers.
Vagrant scents in unsettled air
escape,
to drift in slow motion whirls.
Inside the pale cave
of the shadow-blue shell
all is smooth and white
but for traces
of the final parting:
bird from egg.
Silence in blankness
after the ebb and flow
of a delicate life.
Music of green-toned woods,

of falling water,
has left behind
a fragment of sky
taken gently
and dropped
among withered petals;
a bird's egg,
shell empty.

—SUSAN T., AGE 17

moon
like a silver
flower shineing
through the
fog

Night and the Moon

Night

Children's responses to darkness and night-time range from feelings of coziness and safety to uneasiness, awe, fear. There is a mystery about the onset of night and about night itself. In broad daylight, we can conjure up night, there behind our eyes. This is possible because our amazing minds can ring us anything we wish to "see" and "hear."

Let's see what dark night scenes are alive behind the clear eyes of children. First of all, we need to imagine an absolutely pitch dark night. We cannot see a thing. Can we feel something? Is there a sound?

What can you feel in the dark night? Think of words that let you experience a nighttime feeling. Can we hear night sounds? In the city the night is filled with sounds. In the country, too. What are some city sounds? Put them on the chalkboard, or fill sheets of paper with night words.

How does a siren sound in the night? Can you see the sound of a siren against the black night? Does the sound of the siren have a color? Is it a soft sound? a stabbing sound? What is night made of? Think of night as a kind of cloth. What can the sound of a siren do to the cloth of night? Imagine the sounds of a windy night. How do they differ from the sounds of a still night? With ten words, Randy describes the sounds of night in the following poem:

A DARK WINDY NIGHT
The boat whistle blew . . .
a flower snapped . . .
A door slammed!

—RANDY, AGE 8

The whole fourth-grade class thought about night and painted this word picture of a Minnesota sky:

Pepper and stars
in the
black-winged night.
My hands touch
owl feathers . . .

Suppose we imagine night to be a person. Is it a man? a woman? What kind of clothes does night wear? Imagine what those clothes look like. Do they cling to the body? Do they float behind night? Are night's hands doing something? night's fingers? What kind of hair does night have? What kind of eyes? Are they open? What is night doing? Is night dreaming? Is night on foot? Flying? Riding? What is being ridden? Can you see any packages or baskets? What colors do you imagine night prefers? Black? What are other names for night's favorite color?

In Terry's poem, night is portrayed as a person:

As I went to bed
I heard a noise.
It was the Night Wizard!
You could hear him SWISHING
across the trees!

—TERRY, AGE 10

Night, a giant
eating the sun!

—JENNY, AGE 10

Maybe night is a place. Brian sees it as an alley, "long and narrow." In Anne's poem, the clock "snores midnight" in the "vacant room" of night. In her poem, night becomes a person who "swirls his black cape":

The alley of night
is long and narrow
you hear clocks tick
you see stars in the
black sky

you hear crickets
in your
    sleep

—BRIAN, AGE 9

NIGHT
I wake in the vacant room of night,
The clock snores midnight,
The time of ghosts. I hear the scream
of night, the stars flame, night swirls
his black cape, scrapes the planets.
Noises shatter the night, footsteps of
night fade in the wind, dawn draws
near.

—ANNE, AGE 9

Cathy shows us a special night and scares us on Halloween. Boo!

HALLOWEEN NIGHT
The spooks in the
    night spill shadows
    against the wall. The
    clocks strike midnight.
Ghosts pop out of vacant
    rooms. In the alley
    the breathless moon
    shines and owls howl.

—CATHY, AGE 9

Think of night as an animal. What animals seem to have a
night feeling about them? How does this animal, night, move?
What is happening as the animal comes across the day world?
How does day react? Can night come as a bird? What insect could

be night? In the poems that follow, you will see what kinds of animals occurred to a group of children as they stretched their
minds' nets to capture a new picture of night:

DARKNESS
Every day, after the sun goes down,
a new life begins.
It starts as smoothly as a snake,
as silently as a cat
with her green eye glistening.
Slowly,
        smoothly,
It stalks its prey.
Suddenly it comes—
the other life:
        NIGHT.

—KIM, AGE 11

Did you know
that there is a black bear
in the sky?
And when he roars,
it makes a sound
like thunder.
But he only does it
at night.

—JEFF, AGE 8

Night is like
A black panther
Waiting
for food.

—RANDY, AGE 8

Lorri asks a question. Maybe she is thinking about the panther in Randy's poem:

Where does the panther live
in the dark night of sparks?
Please tell me where he stays
in the moonlight.

—LORRI, AGE 9

Can you see Lorri's "dark night of sparks"? Are those sparks stars? Or is there a fire? What do you see?

The next two poems, which show us night's arrival, also seem to animate night. Mary Beth's poem has an ominous tone to it.

GLOOMY BLACK NIGHT
I felt something
crouching in the dark velvet sky.
I heard the owls hooting,
and a black cat hissing.
I could feel my heart's drumbeat
and the winds howling.
I felt night creeping on.

—MARY BETH, AGE 10

It comes.
The owl awakes from its sleep.
He lets out a cry of fear;
Suddenly the hawks
Rise out of the fields
They all know what's coming—
Night!

—JANET, AGE 11

When night is the subject, many unusual images emerge. Here is an excerpt from Janet's poem "Night Walking":

. . . Velvety darkness
all around me,
the moon,
splendored with beauty . . .

—JANET, AGE 11

Splendored is a word that simply occurred to Janet, and it is just right as she has used it here. Is *splendored* a word? It is now!

In her poem, Elvira thought of the sky and its stars and compared them with a daisied meadow:

In the night,
the sky is clear,
with white shooting-stars,
like a meadow would be
with crystal-white daisies
in the lonely green grass.

—ELVIRA, AGE 10

Most of us have had the experience, just before falling asleep, of a sliding sensation, as though the bed—with us as a passenger—is moving. Margie writes about this strange feeling:

The beds move in the night
When everybody is asleep.
The farmer's house
feels funny
because it is such a
black night!

—MARGIE, AGE 8

Nancy's poem begins with the dark, lights up, and then goes dark again. The device of beginning and ending a poem with the same idea—sometimes with the very same word—is one that children enjoy. It gives a completed feeling to a poem and can solve the ever present problem of all poets: How can I end it?

> Darkness filled the air
> Suddenly it came:
> An enormous lamp lighted
> the sky.
> The darkness was gone!
> Then through the still night
> Came the clouds,
> Covering the moon,
> Darkness returned.
>
> —NANCY, AGE 10

George wrote a poem that seems to move rapidly from beginning to end:

> As the moon came up
> behind a tree,
> a coyote howled,
> a gun fired,
> and a falling star blinded me
> as it raced into the night.
>
> —GEORGE, AGE 11

What gives this poem such speed? Perhaps this rapidity is achieved by relating several events, all happening at once: the moon is rising; we hear a coyote; a gun is shot; and we see a star fall. And look at the strong words George has used to show us that star. He says it *blinded* him as it *raced* into the night. He used those exact words to create a particular effect. He could have described the star as *bright,* and it could have *gone* into the night. Think how much dimmer *bright* would have made the star and how much slower it would have moved had the word *gone* been used instead of *raced.* When you help your children to conjure up the night, don't forget to ask for words like George's to put on your chalkboard or paper.

You need to keep pressing for another, another, and yet another good word that means the same as whatever you are speaking about. As we've found again and again, children's vocabularies abound with words they know but seldom use. By the time they've been fluent speakers for a number of years, their self-expression becomes as commonplace and dull as ours. So, encourage them at an early age to quarry imaginative words and phrases. Everyone is excited when jewels of little-used speech are discovered and put on display for all to admire and use.

Continue to ask for words and more words. And continue to ask questions to draw out children's ideas. Ask questions about sound, sight, color; ask questions like those mentioned in this chapter and throughout the book. Ask the questions of yourself and your children, and encourage the children to question themselves and each other.

The Moon

Even now, with the astronauts' footsteps in its dust, the moon holds a fascination for the earthbound. As its shape changes, as it seems to sail across our night skies, the moon's magic remains.

When you evoke the moon's mystery with children, start with the moon as we know it, as we see it from earth. Then, perhaps, you will want to explore the moon's image from a different perspective—from a spaceship or a moonwalk.

Ask questions that will provoke the children's imagination. Put moon words on the chalkboard or on a sheet of paper. Begin with shapes. What words mean *round*? What things are round? What things are both round and flat? Can a moon be compared with any of these things? If the moon is round like a ball, what is it made of? What metal? What jewel?

Is the moon always round? Do we ever see the whole moon? Think of the moon as it changes from night to night. Can you see the half-moon? What does it remind you of? what else? What does it look like when it is rocking on its curved edge? What are some words that mean the same as *curve*?

If you could have the moon, what would you do with it? Could you hold it in your hand? What would you do with half a moon? with a slice of moon? Think of the thinnest slice of moon you can imagine. What else is so thin and curved? The moon in one of its phases is the subject for this poem:

THE CRADLE
The moon is a cradle
swaying back and forth.
Inside the cradle
is a little baby star.
I guess it has fallen
from the sky.
I think I should give it back
to its mother.
Don't you?

—JANE, AGE 7

Do you know that the moon can move the oceans? How does the moon do this? What does the push and pull of gravity look like? What does gravity feel like to the ocean? A California nine-

year-old used her experience with the moon's pull on the sea to
write this poem:

> The water goes
> splish-splash
> on the rocks,
> And then the sea goes down
> When the moon comes up.
>
> —MARNELL S., AGE 8

What color is the moon—yellow? What are some other words
for the yellow color of the moon? Is the moon always yellow?
What other colors might it be? What color would it be on a summer night, a winter night, a stormy night, a clear night? Is the
moon burning? What color are its flames? Do you ever see the
moon during the day? What does it look like then?

The night Sky
carries
a basket of light.
It Spills stars into my
pocket. Moon beams carry me
into the sky!
by Everybody
Pennington poet E.p.

See all the ways children have expressed the moon's color in the following poems:

The white satin moon
shines down on the ice,
the silver snow.
The black wind
carries the snow
from
tops of trees.

—JENNIFER, AGE 10

The moon is yellow
As can be.
It's the color of gold.
It looks like a golden locket
Hanging from the blue neck
Of the blue shady sky.

—ELVIRA, AGE 10

There is a golden moon tonight
and all the stars
are shining bright.
Her eyes glitter
like stars in space,
and her hands and feet
are the galaxies.

—EDITH S., AGE 9

Edith's moon is bright and golden, but it is also a beautiful lady with glittering eyes and twinkling hands and feet. Could the moon be a person? What would the moon as a person look like? What would its personality be?

Here's a poem with a golden moon—but with a difference:

The moon reminds me
of golden butter.
It looks bright yellow,
And when the stars come out
at night,
They start
  Nibbling
    on
      it!

—GAYNELL M., AGE 8

Barry saw a stretch of moonlight on a rug and wrote this discovery poem:

When I was walking
To the door,
There sat the moon
Glowing with gold.
Now I know it is red,
and blue,
and the color
of my floor!

—BARRY McC., AGE 8

And here is another moon color:

When it is night
the moon is an ivory ball.
The owls sit on trees
and stare at him
with their great big eyes.

—DAN, AGE 12

Jon thinks about night, and comes up with a totally original concept. He speaks about the "house of night" in his poem:

> The snowy stars hung
> in the house of night,
> and snow was shining
> in the moonlight.
> The moon was
> held up
> on velvet
> strings.
> Cold birds fly
> on icy wings.
>
> —JON, AGE 12

When Katie sees the moon, she hears music:

> NIGHT MOON
> I looked outside my window
> and saw the round face
> over my head.
> The freckles of light
> danced over the face.
> I could hear crickets
> playing in their dazzling
>   new orchestra.
> The owls were hooting
> in their choir.
>
> —KATIE, AGE 12

That's what the moon looks like from earth. What if you could travel to it? What words describe the speed of a vehicle as it hurtles through black space? On the chalkboard or on a sheet of paper, put all the words that mean the same as *fly*. How do you describe weightlessness? What appears through the porthole of your spaceship?

What does the moon look like from a distance? How does its appearance change as you get closer and closer? You're there! What words describe the texture of the moon's surface? How do astronauts move around on the moon's surface?

You've completed your mission, and you're leaving the moon. How does the moon look as you fly away from it? Does it get smaller and smaller? What does it remind you of?

After the initial word-finding sessions, we decided to write each poem in three sections: blast-off, spaceflight, and moon walk. However, we did each section as a separate exercise so everyone could really concentrate on that phase of their space adventure. This concentration paid off, as you will see. Notice how each section of every poem has used words that evoke the particular event being described:

BLAST-OFF
Fire!
Ground vibrates—steam—
rocket fuel burns red flame.
It's an earthquake with hot lava—
furnace.

SPACEFLIGHT
Freezing—
soundproof . . . endless.
White clouds swirling, earth blue
—silver stars burn across black—
Freezing.

MOON WALK
Deep holes
dark. Jumping
and fooling around—floating
—silver light glows in the dark—
slowly.

　　　　　　　　　　　　—TOM G., AGE 10

Tom speaks of space as "Freezing." Yet he tells us that "silver stars burn across black," allowing us to imagine icy space filled with burning hot suns that are stars.

BLAST-OFF
Countdown,
high hopes, tense faces . . .
Blast off! Vibrating sounds
drowning out frightening screams—
Breathtaking.

SPACE TRAVEL
Cheetah in the dark
travels to its quest
faster than sound—
whizzing through space—
only the soundless stars
seep through the darkness.

MOON WALKING
Slow-motion elephants
Kicking up dirt
and leaving huge footprints
in the midnight crystals.

　　　　　　　　　　　—SUE VAN D., AGE 12

Sue could have called "midnight crystals" black dust, but that description wouldn't have been as effective.

BLAST-OFF
. . . two, one
Blast Off!
Viewers watch the thrilling dive
to the moon,
Breathlessly
they await
the landing rocket.

SPACE FLIGHT
Diving through space
zooming across the black,
airless sky,
the burning moon,
sparkling stars
look bigger.

MOON WALK
Meadows of black dust
cover the moon.
Astronauts
take great bounds
through craters
filled with silver rain.

—PATTIE VAN D., AGE 10

The strong, unusual images in this poem are "airless sky," "burning moon," "meadows of black dust," and the stunning word picture of "craters filled with silver rain."

ROCKET
Vibrates—
earthquake rumble
red yellow orange fire
red flames—flares—writes like white steam
a pen.

FALLING STARS
Silver
sparkling like
golden stars—falling like
cotton balls softly floating down.
Silent.

MOON WALK
Walking
over hills of
green cheese in their gray suits
floating in the air and talking—
Drifting.

—JANE G., AGE 8

Jane combines the scientific knowledge of today's space-age child with the old tales about the moon when she impishly speaks of the astronauts "walking over hills of green cheese."

ROCKET
Blast!
The ground shrivels.
It sounds like an earthquake
flares of red, yellow, and orange fly up—
white steam.

OUTER SPACE
Silent,
floating in space,
watching the stars fly by
an infinity of blackness—
silent.

MOON WALK
Sand puffing up
like smoke from a chimney
from the hard shoes that hit the sand.
Moon Walk.

—CAROLINE L., AGE 10

Caroline tells us, "The ground shrivels." *Shrivels* is exactly the right word to show us how fast the earth becomes small as the rocket takes off.

Come back down to earth. The night, the dark, the moon—use them often as subjects for lively, imaginative writing.

The old lady's skin
it is like sandpaper
her mind
it holds a trunk of memories
memories. She opens it every
day. Andy Strong

People and More People

Here is a subject that is without limits; people are everywhere. What makes us what we are? What makes us who we are? Are we alike? how? Are we different? how? What are people all about?

Let's begin by looking at the one person we ought to know best—ourselves. How can you sum yourself up? Can you choose words that will paint a portrait of yourself? Start by asking the children to ask questions about themselves. Encourage them to find creative ways to express the person they know best.

This is Julie's self-portrait in haiku form. What kind of girl do you see here?

> A bee has this mouth,
>> feeling sorry for herself—
>>> a bad time of day.

—JULIE C., AGE 10

Cathy tells us what she is in this next poem. Look at the marvelous variety of images she uses to bring us closer to her portrait:

> I am a tall birch tree
> with branches beginning to bend.
> I am a small dog
> with a coat beginning to shine.
> I am Spring
> just beginning to come forth,
> And I am a freshly oiled door
> beginning to slowly open.

—CATHY C., HIGH SCHOOL

Sometimes it is hard at first for children or young people to get a handle on which way to describe themselves. They know so many things about themselves, but they need help with focusing their self-knowledge so that their poems can become concrete, creative works, rather than general "I am" listings.

One way to begin is to ask questions like these: What creature in the animal kingdom reminds you of yourself? What characteristics do you have that are like those of an animal, a bird, an insect?

Betsy is a nine-year-old with the creative ability to feel the stretch, and pull, and length of a giraffe's neck. She has obviously had some experience with sore throats as well.

> I
> am a giraffe.
> When I get
> a sore throat,
> It hurts
> 　　ten
> 　　　　feet
> 　　　　　　down.
> It's a L O N G
> swallow!
>
> 　　　　　　　—BETSY A., AGE 9

Two girls who see themselves as chatterers chose two very different animals for comparisons:

> I feel I would be a monkey . . .
> I would swing my tail. I would
> chatter and chatter all the time. A
> chattering monkey is what I would want to be!
>
> 　　　　　　　—RAE, AGE 9

> It seems to me
> that I am a parakeet.
> I like to talk
> and chatter
> like
> 　　a
> 　　　　parakeet.
>
> 　　　　　　　—MARLENE, AGE 10

David tells us this:

I'd like to be
a dog.
Ar-r-r-r-r-
-arr-r-r-r.
I will walk noisy.
I'll bark at people
and
BITE
them!
I will eat Terry dog food . . .
Yum-yum-yum-m-m . . .
I will look mean.

      —DAVID M., AGE 8

David took evident pleasure in putting together the letters that would stand for the menacing growl of a dog. The poem is interesting since David's good nature and mild manner were famous in the third grade classroom that year. None of us knew that he wanted to be so ferocious. Sometimes people discover things they didn't know they knew about themselves when they begin to write self-portraits.

  Have you ever had the feelings Katie is describing in this poem?

Sometimes
I feel like a turtle
walking on the sand
or a snail
inching along.
Sometimes

I feel so lazy
that I could just trip
over anything
that is before me.
It would be
so hard
   to
      pick
        up
          a
           pin.

—KATIE, AGE 11

Another myself-as-a-turtle poem comes to us from Maria R. of Micronesia:

THE TURTLE
(A poem of myself)

A turtle that has been short of air
In the depth of the ocean,
Struggling madly,
Kicking against water,
Trying to come up
For another supply
Of oxygen.
But he can't
For one of his legs has been caught
By a giant clam
Far down the depth
Of the vast ocean.

—MARIA R., AGE 17

It is a powerful poem, with strong words to show us the breathless, choking panic of the animal. The closing lines, "Far down the depth/Of the vast ocean," seem to pull us down, down with the turtle itself.

After your students have spent some time painting themselves with words, ask them to paint word pictures of their friends. When they have finished, ask for volunteers to read their word portraits to the class. Have the class guess who is being described.

Mitsuo S. was one of the members of the Micronesian class whose poems you have been reading. Two of his classmates used him as subject matter when they were asked to write a character study. What kind of picture do you see when you combine the two impressions of Mitsuo?

MITSUO
Silence dwells in him always
but once a word parts the two attached lips,
you can hardly remain unlaughing.
Slowness is always maintained in his walk,
Kindness and generosity can be read clearly on
     the face,
Wherever this slim and slender clown walks,
There is apt to be laughter.

—MARIA R., AGE 17

And now, see him through different eyes:

     Slim, slender and tall like a mast of a
          schooner.
     And swaying side to side, back and forth as
          he moves,
     His aloha, waving smoothly as a sail
          fastened to the mast.

M His voice, deep and low, attracts the crew.
i   He enjoys the happiness and the worth of
t   life,
s   And in him there is no seriousness, almost,
u But the kind Nature has given him the spell
o   To calm the fierce tiger,
And alter the silence of the world.

—MASAHARU, AGE 19

The affectionate regard of Maria and of Masaharu for their class-
mate is obvious. These descriptions were so apt, as a matter of
fact, that when the poems were originally read, without titles, the
class had no hesitation in shouting, "Mitsuo!"

Mitsuo, too, wrote a character study. This one is untitled, but
it is obviously a description of a strong, dominant man. In the last
line, the word *you* puts the reader directly in the path of this man:

Come the typhoon, come the fire,
What he says never changes.
Roaring of electric power-plant,
Noises created by the crowd of the whole world:
People playing on the farthest end of the earth
Have no difficulty hearing his voice when he talks.
Tight . . . hard . . . twisted,
He comes toward you with shadows of muscles.

—MITSUO, HIGH SCHOOL

When Ulai uses the word *queer* in the next poem, she means
crazy, silly, or acting foolish:

M. LEERNGOF
Obese, bulgy, plump,
She is an elephant.

She is more queer than more serious.
When the world is in silence,
She can converse it into noisiness.
While she is serious, she causes laughter,
when she is queer, she causes seriousness.
But after the gleam of glee,
she is all discouraged and gloomy.

—ULAI, AGE 16

Kelly sums up her friend Charlene for us in just four lines:

CHARLENE
fearlessly laughing
she wraps the world in humor
and drops the pink-bowed thing
into her pocket.

—KELLY, HIGH SCHOOL

Here is a cinquain, a character study in just five lines:

Laurie
has thumb in mouth
In a world of her own
Blaming people for her mistakes:
Laurie.

—DEBBIE, AGE 13

Writing a character study in cinquain has the same advantages that writing other cinquains on other subjects has. The restricted form forces the writer to look for exactly the right words, to focus in on specifics that present a succinct word portrait.

Here is Mary's portrait of her friend Ann:

Ann
A tuning fork of feathers
On which the slightest breeze
May play a single note
That rings, reverberates
and stings my face with tenderness.

(She loves her world away.)

Sudden!
Treftings crash
Apart and
Must be Puzzled together
Transcintly.

A tuning fork of feathers.

—MARY, AGE 16

Like the words in Lewis Carroll's "The Jabberwocky," *treftings* and *transcintly* are not part of our vocabularies. But, in Mary's study of Ann, we are able to read them with some understanding of their meaning. At least they don't get in the way of the essential picture of Ann as a "tuning fork of feathers."

Alison wrote about Jane one summer:

Jane's hair—
soft and wet.
Pearls of light raindrops
on each strand of hair
when she is walking
through the rain.

—ALISON, AGE 11

Not a character study, really, but it is a skillful use of words by a young girl to describe her friend "when she is walking through the rain."

Not only our friends but members of our own families can sit for their word portraits. Think about people who live in your house—the people you see most and, perhaps, know best. What words can you use to sum up your mother, your father, your brothers and sisters? Can you think of a single characteristic that defines each of your family members? Try this exercise at home, for fun. It works as a "mystery game" at parties—and turns out to be a good-natured icebreaker.

Many people have pet expressions that they say again and again. Some people use their hands in certain characteristic ways. We recognize some by their posture. These are the kinds of special *noticings* we can do when trying to realize a person's image accurately in words. Judge for yourself whether the essential inner qualities of Tosiwo's father come out in this next poem:

MY FATHER
His words are sacred to me.
He shoots with love, but nobody can see it.
The earth is revolving,
but his words are straight as a sword to me.
People think he is only a man. However,
I consider him as the only man who has two
    hearts,
One for blood circulation, and one for love.
           —TOSIWO, AGE 17

Roxanne found many moods to speak of when she decided to describe her brother:

MY BROTHER
My brother is like stones
Dropping on glass
When he is angry.
If he is mean like a whip,
He cuts.
He is like a piece
Of wood
Or a goofy clown
When he feels lazy,
Or like smooth fishes swimming.
When nice,
He is like a soft pillow
You rest your head on.
Asleep, he is like
soft droning
(Except, he SNORES!)
That is my brother:
Nice, kind, mean, angry
sleeping
and awake.

—ROXANNE, HIGH SCHOOL

Here is Joe's cinquain portrait of his brother:

Brother:
Friend? Enemy?
Someone you can talk to.
Big and strong like a gorilla.
My friend.

—JOE, AGE 12

In her description of a child, Sylvia is looking back toward a time when she was small:

Towering dreamland,
Transcending dandylions,
I encircled all for my menagerie.
From tablespoon minnows
dressed in sequins
decorating my jovial creek
to my grass geysers
caressing my chocolated
earth cake,
All was mine,
crisp and free.
Now my record player
sings my tune.

—SYLVIA, HIGH SCHOOL

Sylvia's extravagant language reminds me of "Fern Hill," a poem of childhood by Dylan Thomas, whose use of words for their color, their sound, their shape on the tongue appeals to children as well as adults.

Here is another childhood remembered by a fifth grader looking back:

Shoe laces
Like snakes
Squirming.
They try to get
Away,
Squirming
Out of
My

Fingertips.
I am four.

—LISA, AGE 10

A roomful of fourth graders thought about what it might be like to grow old. We filled our sheets of paper with the same tapestry of words I wrote on the chalkboard.

Jenny imagined a person's time on earth running out, and she has given us a memorable image—a countdown—without actually spelling this out. Poetry is *clues*, when it is at its best!

I dreamed
I opened a
door and
numbers
began to
count
   down
      slowly to
        one.

—JENNY, AGE 10

When we talked about the things that people do during their lives, many activities and some occupations went up on the board, and on our collections of words on sheets of paper. After the board was erased, the children had the words to work from.

Garden was one of those words. An ordinary word, but look at the magic Alisa has worked with it!

A garden full of memories
you can pick up and smile at.
You plant your childhood
in your dreams.

The seeds spill into voices
they bloom into daffodils
when the sun beats down
on shiny memories.

—ALISA, AGE 9

Notice what Susan does with the idea of a closet.

Gray rooms,
Musty odors.
An empty closet
with calling voices
of my children.
        Come back!

—SUSAN, AGE 9

With the words *ladder* and *knit* on their papers and up on the chalkboard, these fourth graders had no trouble turning ordinary concepts into small miracles. Here is one:

Old age
creeps up on her.
She knits
a ladder of memories—
memories
of her husband.
She wants
to climb the ladder
to her husband,
to the window
of the night.

—DAVID, AGE 9

Looking at photographs and paintings of people is another good way to motivate the writing of character studies. Julie, a sixth grader, wrote about Cézanne's painting *Victor Chocquet:*

> Stern, but gentle. A man with a touch of a grin. Not a political man. But a log cabin man. He gets very vulgar at times. But other times wonderful words come from the mouth. He is not stunning in his old age, and he does not try to be Dashing to impress us.
>
>   —JULIE C., AGE 10

After studying the painting *Helle Babbe, Witch of Haarlem* by the Dutch painter Frans Hals, an eighth grade girl wrote this analysis of the strange-looking woman:

> She sits alone, hissing and cursing at other people. Her owl stands over her like the devil. Her face is aged with her problems and her meanness. When she smiles, all you see is black; teeth are gone. With her beery, winey breath she goes around sneaking behind other people's backs. But as the clock strikes the magical hour, she gets a certain wild and ferocious feeling growling in her. She cannot control her rage. It's boiling in her! She is going mad!
>
>   —DEBBIE, AGE 13

Farmer's Wife by Grant Wood gave Jennifer her idea for a word portrait. The painting shows only an elderly lady, with a farm behind her, sitting and holding a sansevieria in a clay pot:

THE HAPPY, LONELY LADY
    Boiling, steaming sun staring me right in the eyes. I'm all alone. But I have lots of things that mean so much to

me. I have my house and the plant that my husband
planted for me before he died. This living plant will keep
me living with pride.

—JENNIFER, AGE 13

These fifth grade boys could call on their imaginations to "become ninety years old." They wrote their poems from inside the
feelings and perceptions of a person who is at the opposite end of
life from themselves.

Alone
in the house
all night long.
TV on.
Alone.
Wind blowing,
leaves hiding the windows.
Nervous.
Alone.

—LEE, AGE 10

Memories swinging, running!
Everybody was a child once.
I love children.
I know I am climbing up
in age
and life stops.
The lights turn off.

—MIKE, AGE 10

In the books we read, we come to know characters through
the words authors use to describe them. When a writer tells us

that an old lady "extends her claw" to pick up a little cake, we have an immediate reaction to her: she is not going to be a gentle, soft, loving character in the story.

Writers can give clues to people's characters and personalities just by describing their body movements. With this in mind, I asked the children to reach into the mystery box and choose a slip of paper from it. Each paper contained a short statement about a person. The children were to write a description showing us how this person moves about.

Julie's mystery slip said: "This fearful little person is afraid of everything." Julie's description tells us who this little person is:

> A flittering little girl who is in the corner and hides
> every time someone passes. When walking, she slips on
> her heel or toe. She has her head in her arms, too!
> —JULIE, AGE 10

Jennifer, age twelve, created a character from the same mystery slip in just one short clause, ". . . and when I said 'hi' she shriveled up in a ball and started to cry."

Tina picked the mystery slip "The General arrives."

> The General arrives. He walks like an elephant and
> never is polite. His head swings like an elephant with a
> headache and he trumpets out orders.
> —TINA, AGE 12

Tina's portrait is a fine example of the consistent use of a simile. The general does, indeed, seem "like an elephant," with head swinging (an excellent touch), and his orders trumpeted out.

George's mystery slip read: "A robber comes around the corner."

He slinks around the corner with the cunning of a
snake ready to strike.

—GEORGE, AGE 12

Using the same mystery slip, Anne described a different thief:

The thief was slinking back into the dark, mysterious
alley. You could faintly hear the clod of his feet as he
stealthily crept away. He stumbled, staggered, and fell
into the trap.

—ANNE, AGE 12

Rita's slip of paper read, "The clowns are coming." Her little
piece begins with an *-ing* word that immediately starts us off in
the direction Rita wants us to go:

Jumping, twirling into the tent, making funny and
weird noises, the clowns came.

—RITA, AGE 10

Other mystery slips that day included these: "A tired nurse
tries to do her job." "A businesslike teacher gets her room ready."
"The bully comes out to the playground." "The witch comes down
the dark stairway." "A farmer drives a load of hay home in the
cool evening." "A construction worker looks up in time to see a
rope break." "A firefighter rushes to find equipment when the
alarm goes off."

Writers often choose names for their characters so that we
can see them more clearly. Charles Dickens named a character
Uriah Heep. That is a name that makes us see—what? What kind
of names would you give to a town drunk, a college professor, a
piano teacher, a pretty teacher, a fat banker, and a poor old man?

Jennifer gave those characters these names:

college professor—Prof. Everett
pretty teacher—Mrs. Trotta
fat banker—Mr. Bergantail
poor old man—Mr. Nelson

And Tina's list was quite different, of course:

college professor—Prof. Willdle
piano teacher—Mrs. Dollarson
pretty teacher—Miss Kathy Bronson
fat banker—Harry Bette
poor old man—Charlie Wilson

In both lists there are some excellent names—names that make us see a person. Which teacher do you think is prettier, Mrs. Trotta or Miss Kathy Bronson? Which is the poorer old man, Mr. Nelson or Charlie Wilson? Of the two fat bankers, which seems the fattest, Mr. Bergantail or Harry Bette? It's an interesting exercise and one that never fails to involve the children's imaginations.

You can also give a character's name and ask children to describe that person. For example, who is Henry Glockaspear? Marilyn was sure she knew him and described him this way:

Henry Glockaspear is a middle-age square. He's really hung up on Bach, Beethoven, and Mozart. He has black hair with a gray streak. He wears spectacles that hang on the tip of his nose. His clothes are old-fashioned and he hates children very much.

—MARILYN, AGE 13

Can you imagine someone who is named Mrs. Beulah Umpar? Jennifer can:

... Delightful, nice old lady. Owns apartment
house ... gray hair ... always laughing ... she wears old
fashion clothes, tries to understand the world ... friends
to everyone ...

—JENNIFER, AGE 13

Thirteen-year-old Debbie sees a character named Sally Blad-
den as "ugly with warts (spoiled) ... red hair ... hazel eyes ... a
mean baby sitter ... 13 years old."

Meet Miss Millie Pinter. What kind of person does your imagination show you? Notice the sounds in her name. How do they
suggest a different character from the sounds that the name *Beulah Umpar* suggests? Is there such a thing as a heavy name? A
lightweight name?

MISS MILLIE PINTER
Fluttering, continually fluttering ...
Now flitting over to examine a flower.
Flying on feet
as light as feathers
Darting about
seeing and hearing ...
Everything.
Similar to a chickadee:
never resting.

—SUEBEE, AGE 11

The name *Miss Millie Pinter*, with its short *i* sounds, reminded
the young poet of light, quick actions and images. Wouldn't a
character named Mrs. Beulah Umpar need an entirely different
description? The sounds in her name are slow and heavy. Say
them and see how they hit your ear and your imagination.

We have met many people on these pages. We have seen self-portraits in this gallery. We have seen portraits of friends and relatives. People have come to life because of words! Ideas can come from everywhere.

Use paintings, portraits, and self-portraits, as I have suggested in this chapter. You can also use photographs from home, photos of children and elderly people, photos of crowds and close-ups of faces in crowds, photos of well-known people in a particular mood, photos from newspapers and magazines. Have your children write sketches like the ones in this chapter. Have them become the person in the picture as they write. Or they can be observers writing about the picture.

Pick names from literature that the children are not familiar with. Have them write descriptions of the characters who bear those names. Then compare the children's descriptions with how the author originally conceived of the characters. Or have the children read descriptions of characters from literature and then name those characters. Then compare their names with the original names the author chose for the characters.

Write descriptions of TV characters in terms of the way the actors' movements and attitudes make us believe in their personalities. Imagine a TV character portrayed by a different actor. How would the new actor have to change his or her ways of walking, gesturing, speaking?

People and more people! Find them and show them to us. Words, will be the brush, the camera, the tools to make us see— people.

Inside an alligator's
        dark,
            dark,
                dark,
mouth is like a
        cave
without any lights - or
an endless tunnel.

Animal Fair

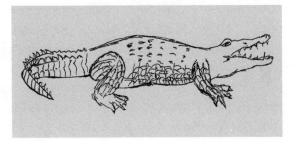

I went to the Animal Fair," starts an old rhyme by an unknown author, "and the birds and the beasts were there. . . ." The birds and the beasts are here, too—in a whole chapter of word pictures done by children and young people.

In the last chapter we explored writing about people, all kinds and varieties of people. We noted that in describing people, their attitudes, gestures, speech patterns, variety in clothing, names, and other attributes distinguish one person from others.

But describing an animal can become more difficult. We need to think carefully about each word that will help the reader see our animals better. We need to search out colorful words that will let the reader feel the massive weight and sway of an elephant, the lightness and bounce of a kitten, an alley cat's prowl, the soar and drop of a fish hawk. We need also to search for words to distinguish one elephant from another. We need to look for a way to tell our readers that we are describing one particular kitten, rather than all kittens. All of these creatures differ from one another, and the writer must work skillfully to show these differences.

Let's talk about the ways in which poets decide just what word is most appropriate for their special needs. If we are describing a tiny animal that moves quickly, we need to look for words that move quickly, too. We've already mentioned the relative speeds of words, how the sound of the word we use can suggest the meaning we want to convey. The word *quick* has a short *i* sound followed by a staccato consonant sound; it moves rapidly as we say it. On the other hand, the word *slow* sounds and moves much less rapidly because of the long vowel sound.

Fill the chalkboard or paper with a snowstorm of animal-movement words. Ask your children how tiny animals move. What do they look like? Ask for fast, tiny-sounding words like *skitter* and *scurry.* How many words can they think of that mean the same as running fast and lightly? How does an elephant move? An ox? Ask for heavy words like *lumbering* and *wallow* and *stomp.* How does a leopard move? Ask for powerful-sounding words like *pounce, swoop, thrust,* or *spring.*

You might call out the names of animals, birds, insects, sea creatures and let the children provide words for each one until the board or paper is filled and the word supply is exhausted. Use a book that describes all kinds of animals from the most familiar to the most exotic. If no one knows exactly what a certain animal is like, show a picture of it and give the pertinent facts: where it lives, what it eats, how it defends itself. It's fun to introduce yourself to a new animal by trying to find the exact words to describe it. When you've finished, you will have a menagerie of words to start ideas exploding into lively writing.

Coleen thought about a swan, concentrated on all of the most swanlike characteristics she could call to mind, and came up with a piece of writing that seemed to her classmates to be an accurate, imaginative picture. Do you agree?

SWAN

The swan thrashed her webbed pads behind her in the swirling water. She went gliding across the lake like a leaf glides to the ground in a soft wind.

Then, she waddled onto the shore and across the waving grass. Then, turning around, she swept back to the shore and the swirling water, where the swan again floated in peace on the lake.

—COLEEN, AGE 15

Is *thrashed* a good choice for the action of the swan's feet? Do you like "webbed pads" better than "webbed feet"? Is the comparison between the swan's glide and a leaf's glide a good one? Do you like the contrast between the gliding swan in the water and the waddling swan on the shore? How would you write a piece about a swan?

FEATHER TREE
Shimmering
the water reflects
ringlets of light

onto the feathery tree
on the shore.
One brown duck
swims under the tree.
Smoothly gliding along,
she joins
the rest of the ducks.

—JANE E., AGE 11

Jane's primary interest—her motivation for writing—was the play of light on a narrow-leafed mountain ash in the fall. The slim leaves of mountain ash are arranged along a central stem, and each branch does seem to be made of feathers. The image "ringlets of light" shows an intuitive sense of language, used with grace and ease.

If you have ever watched a heron standing absolutely motionless in the water, waiting for a fish, you will appreciate the power of the image in the next poem.

HERON
A statue stands motionless on knobby stilts.
Nothing stirs but her plumage startled by the
        wind.
Slowly, slowly one eye opens—
Then a steely needle flashes, burning the water.
Silence returns without a sound to hurt it.
A statue stands motionless on knobby stilts . . .

—MARY C., HIGH SCHOOL

Mary has obviously observed this bird with great interest, and her picture is stunning in its accuracy. The piece begins with all movement suspended. Only plumage "stirs . . . startled by the wind." And then, with the slow opening of an eye, *all* is movement—the beak that "flashes" into the water, the splash we can almost hear and see in our minds as bird stabs fish. The circular form of the whole piece, with the last line repeating the first line exactly, returns us to the vigil of the heron. The ellipsis at the end of the last line was placed there by the poet to show us that it will all begin again.

Anne sees small brown sparrows in a group that seem to be conversing:

SPARROWS
Sparrows sit on the windowsill
gossiping
'til their heads
fall off.

—ANNE, AGE 11

THE BIRD
Time is irrelevant to
    my blazing, yellow and
    boisterous
        clock.
He sings his song
    to the day,
caring not—what
    I say.

—MARY M., HIGH SCHOOL

We don't know exactly what kind of bird we see here, but we have a clue that tells us he is a true early bird.

Eagles are, understandably, a favorite subject for writers. When Joseph actually saw an eagle high in a northern Minnesota sky, he wrote a spur-of-the-moment poem:

I saw an eagle in the sky
flying so free and high.
I wish I could join him
in his dance
in the sky.

—JOSEPH, AGE 13

When he brought it to the group and read it aloud, there were some carefully considered criticisms from the other youngsters. And Joseph had to rethink his work. Everyone agreed that "his dance in the sky" was an unusual and fitting way to describe the bird's flight. They were bothered by "so free and high," since the word *so* does nothing but weaken the expansive feeling of "free and high." *So* can be used successfully to mean *very* only when it is followed by an example. For example, "It is so cold outside" does not express the extent of coldness as well as "It is so cold outside that my breath froze on my eyelashes." In the second sentence, *so* becomes a good tool to tell us exactly how cold, hot, or whatever.

The children also thought, after hearing Joseph read his poem several more times, that "in the sky" in line one was not necessary. They agreed that *high* tells us that the eagle is "in the sky." It turned out, then, that Joseph only had to remove four words! But see how taut and strong his poem becomes with those four words taken out:

I saw an eagle
flying free and high.
I wish I could join him
in his dance in the sky.

—JOSEPH, AGE 13

Another eagle appears in this little scene:

> The eagle peers down from its high perch looking for
> a meal, then swoops down quietly and swiftly and
> clutches its prey.

—EMILY, AGE 10

Emily's choice of words shows her concern for strong images: *peers, swoops, quietly, swiftly,* and *clutches.* These are eagle words.

Look for the descriptive words in this following piece of writing. Can you see the lion, see the flash of light, feel the bullet?

HUNTING SAFARI

At the deepness of the night an old lazy lion curls up. He just settles down and smells something. It goes away . . . and comes again . . . now! It's close! Jumping up, he rushes into a fury of light. Stunned by brightness, he roars. A sharp, stone-like thing hits him! The dark, spooky shadows roam around him . . . He wakes up in the Happy Hunting Ground.

—ANNE, AGE 11

Anne's use of phrases like "stunned by brightness" and "a fury of light" shows us her unusually perceptive ear and a real awareness of the power of the words she chooses. Look at her out-of-the-ordinary "shadows roam." If you will say this phrase aloud several times you will see that it has a low, dark sound appropriate to the description of a dying animal. You'd have a hard time saying "shadows roam" in a quick, lighthearted way, or in a high-pitched voice. Try it.

You can appreciate Anne's eleven-year-old expertise when you realize how *right* her choice of language is in this short piece.

To see what it is we mean by writing creatively, explore Anne's poem and other poems carefully, word by word, with your students.

Steven writes about deer. Then he adds wolves, and ends with the most powerful wolf words he could think of:

OUT IN THE FOREST
Snow falling gently
The wind blowing
in the forest,
the deer running swift.
The wolves attacking
the deer—
The deer leaps over
and into the brush.
The deer runs
fast as it can
from
the scissor jaws.

—STEVEN, AGE 10

Earlier, you met Emily's swooping eagle. Here is her cat:

The cat creeps along lightly and swiftly on its delicate paws, ready to pounce on a mouse.

—EMILY, AGE 10

And here is a mouse:

Ebony streak slinks by—
Luminous eyes search—
Bits of light—

Now she stops—
Crouched, Tense.
    Waiting.

—DEBBY, HIGH SCHOOL

A giraffe stops to have its portrait drawn for us, thanks to Peggy's inner vision and ability to use language in new ways:

GIRAFFE
A brown and gold lattice piece
    summits
    the sky.
The legs
    on four stilts—
    the expanse of earth.
She tongues the leafy growth
    Vaulting
    Racing
    Speeding
    across the savannah.

—PEGGY, HIGH SCHOOL

Look at Peggy's giraffe once again and see the accuracy of the image "brown and gold lattice piece." The word *summits* is another example of a verb made from a word generally used as a noun. *Stilts* has been used twice in this chapter about animal descriptions—first for the heron's legs and now for the giraffe's. Is it an appropriate word in both instances? Is it more suitable and exact in one poem than in the other? Can you improve upon the word in either poem? How? Experiment and see what you can do.

Listen to the sound *umb* in many of the words in the next poem and ask if the repetition of that sound adds to our sense of the characteristics of polar bears. How does it do this? Write some more polar bear words together.

> Polar bears tumble
> with a scurry rumble
> right into a puddle
> while they're in deep slumber
> on a winter's morn.
>
> —RUTH, HIGH SCHOOL

Connie's poems tend to rhyme, and she uses rhyming words in an easy, natural way. This poem has a feeling of stopped action, like a movie of horses suddenly stopped short and held as a still picture for us to see.

DRY SUMMER EVENING
Chestnuts, roans, a black, a bay,
Scattered in the deep dark way.
Heavy hearts because of thirst,
with jagged wounds that should be nursed.
A stallion so willing to fight for his herd,
The watchful lead mare awaiting the word.

> —CONNIE, AGE 10

This poem is from one of the young writers in Micronesia:

OCTOPUS
Sitting on a coral like a coral
Resting on the sand like the sand
With his eight arms spreading out
He catches with stride his food.

The king of all the sea creatures
Soft and flexible body without bones
Yet kills even the giant whale
With his black smoky weapon
And hundreds of suckers on his arms.

But he's afraid of the heavenly phenomena
For when the lightning flashes across the sky
He shall flee and vanish under the coral
And when the thunder roars over him
He holds the coral and shrinks himself.

Each time the thunder rolls and roars
He will break his arms one by one
And when the hunger strikes him at once
He eats his broken arms greedily.

When the thunder is gone and the sky is clear
He sits again on a coral like a coral
With his eight broken arms spreading out
And still he is the king of the sea.

—MASAHARU, AGE 20

Now you've met all the animals in this poetic carnival, this parade of birds and beasts from the Animal Fair as seen by young writers from many places. The common thread that binds all of this writing into a single piece is the poets' interest in words and their power to perform on the page. This willingness to experiment, to sample many words before choosing the best one for the job, is a satisfying result of the no-holds-barred attitude toward language that these young people accepted with enthusiasm and delight.

Have you seen the river dance
over the banks?
Have you seen the river go crazy
and swollow up a town?
Have you seen the river overflow
and climb the high, tall mountains
like a expert climber?
Have you seen the muddy
waters gallop over the long
grassy feilds?

Animating
the Inanimate

In the two previous chapters we have seen that words, used with imagination and skill, can bring to three-dimensional life people, animals, birds, and insects of all kinds. We can show the inner feelings of a person simply by describing a walk, or the tilt of a head; we can give ferocity to a lion, flight to a dragonfly, or lanky-legged height to a giraffe.

All this is accomplished by merely choosing the right words. By this time, it must be evident that words are magical and powerful. We can use them to do our bidding. We can be as powerful ourselves as any wizard!

Writers often write about nonliving, inanimate things as though those things were alive. The American writer Willa Cather, in her novel *O Pioneers*, described old pioneer houses on the prairie as though they were animals—cattle, perhaps:

> The dwelling houses were set about haphazard on the tough prairie sod; some of them looked as if they had been moved in overnight, and others *as if they were straying off by themselves, headed straight for the open prairie* [emphasis added].

It is hard to think of a more effective way to show the reader that small, impermanent Nebraska town than to say the houses looked as though they'd been "moved in overnight" and that some others seemed to be "straying off by themselves" like dumb animals on the prairie.

In "The Clock," we see an inanimate object described as an old man:

THE CLOCK
An old man sits.
Your hands used to go
so fast.
Now they shake
and go
so slowly.

—RITA, AGE 10

Here is another old man. This time we see him in wintry branches stretched against the cold sky:

BRANCHES
Cold, stiff—
like an old man stretching his arms,
trying to get the bitter frost
out of his body.

—DEBBIE, AGE 13

How can you motivate children to look at an inanimate object and see it as something with a life of its own—breathing and alive?

As an example, think of automobiles. What can they remind us of? Put the word *automobiles* on the chalkboard. What living things come to mind when we think of automobiles—animals? What are the animals doing? Do they eat? How? Do they make sounds? What sounds? List as many as you can. Why are these creatures making the sounds? Do they think? What are they thinking? Why? Are there family groups of automobiles? Here is a possible list of words for your chalkboard: *whine, nuzzle, bucking, sleek, blinking, starting, stray, nosing, tracks, crouch, spring, delicate, race, strong.* How can we use these words to describe our animal-automobiles?

Think about a long line of trucks moving along. Here is Debbie's word picture. She uses two animal images to describe her trucks. Is one better than the other? Why? With what animal would you compare this line of trucks?

Truck convoy: like ants following each other, carrying
their food home. Or, like elephants moving along slowly,
stomping and telling everything in their way to move.

—DEBBIE, AGE 13

Think of a highway full of cars at night. Are the headlights eyes? Whose eyes are they? Where do they go? Why do they stop? What do they see? Do they blink? Sally can see them clearly in her imagination:

CARS AT NIGHT
Released from their cages
into a dark . . .
blinking their eyes,
skidding around a corner they go,
bracing the road.

—SALLY A., AGE 13

Put a list of *things* on a piece of paper or a chalkboard and ask the children to choose one or more that appeals to them. For each one chosen, ask the children to make it live, first by giving it human characteristics, and second, animal traits. Your list could include these things and more: old shoes, clock, house, skyscraper, mobile home park, rocks, mountains, scissors, clothes on hangers, clothing on a floor, gloves, mittens, numbers, letters of the alphabet.

Along with a list, you might put names of things on slips of paper to be picked out, one at a time, from the mystery box that we've mentioned in these chapters.

Or have a tableful of actual objects for animating from which interested children can choose. Actually seeing an old boot, an antique satin slipper, a worn pocket watch, or a delicate wristwatch might trigger responses that merely naming the object could not accomplish.

Photographs, too, offer a wide range of possibilities. A picture of eggs in a carton might result in an amusing image. A chair tilted back against a porch wall, a lumpy jacket draped over a railing, a sprightly sailboat slanted against the waves—all these pictures could be idea starters.

Once you begin to think about how you would animate something, the pictures you seek out in magazines and newspapers will find you. You will note possibilities in every photo you see. You might find lines of telephone poles or mounds of grapefruit or oranges in the food advertisements. When you see a picture of twigs, snow-covered bushes huddled on the lawn, or a cluster of flowers nodding in the wind, you'll think, "Why, yes, they could be . . ." Start thinking about animation, and your picture collection will grow apace. Together, you and your children can collect pictures for the gallery of inanimates, as well, and there'll be no stopping the flow of images these pictures will generate.

You and your children may find that animating the inanimate for a while, it will be hard to shake the habit. You will begin to see a personality in every chair you see. (Look! It has knees!) No tool on your garage shelf will remain inanimate.

No soup tureen or soup pot or sugar bowl and lid will ever be content to sit placidly on your kitchen shelf again. Instead, you'll see them as a fat family. The tureen has her hands on her hips, her hair in a bun atop her head; the soup pot, with its big belly and one arm pointing severely, scowls at you now; and the little round sugar bowl folds its fat arms and wishes it could keep its domed hat from sitting askew.

Or, look at a sugar bowl in a totally different way, as Pattie did.

A bird lands
in the kitchen cupboard,
sitting there
with its wings straight,
big belly full.

—Pattie, age 10

Are you a shoe? Carol's shoe is a special shoe, indeed!

CLOWN'S SHOE
Massaging my mouth
with my tongue,
I wear the foot
of a clown
and I clomp around
clumsily on my
big, fat nose!

—CAROL, AGE 10

Thats the Old Ballet Shoe

I was a Pink ballet shoe
I danced and glided
My shoe laces danced.
But now I sit in the front—
Watch the dancers dance.
I yell "Look at me use me please."
But the others laugh
I wish my skin was smooth
Not wrinkled and torn
I miss my friends
But some day my dream will come true!

Mop

Exhausted—
Treated like a punching
        bag
Needs a new face lift.
    Aching all over!

One afternoon, I picked up the kindergarten dust mop and tilted it toward my ear, as though it were whispering something to me. When I asked the children to tell me what the mop was saying, this is what I was told by those five-year-olds:

I will go dancing
with a girl!
At a restaurant,
I will eat spaghetti.
I will brush my hair
and buy a new
yellow suit
and black dancing shoes and
a white tie!

I hope you are willing to risk being haunted by your own possessions. The life with which you and your children imbue these objects is bound to delight you every time. What do you see when you read this poem?

Gleaming eyes
big and black,

following me
from side to side.
Two chimneys
for two ears up high.
A door for his nose.
Sad and lonely in despair—
Poor old house
on a hillside.

—DOROTHY K., AGE 8

Natural phenomena can be animated with great success. Some sort of animal with a huge mouth and claws is being described in this next poem. What do you see?

Today,
Nature swallowed
the sun.
The shore was clawed
with
the prey-seeking
waters.

—NANCY, HIGH SCHOOL

These animals are also frantic to get to the shore:

The rusty tiger-waves pounce to the shore.
Caring for none but themselves,
they leap on each other's backs
trying to get to their prey
where they will gorge themselves
on the sand
and roll back,
satisfied.

—PAT, HIGH SCHOOL

Marilyn writes about the same waves-meet-shore scene, but she sees it altogether differently. Does her image surprise you?

Waves,
like old ladies in white hats
coming home
to the shore—
noisily whispering about . . .
. . . something . . .
what, I don't know.

—MARILYN, AGE 13

Night is always an exciting subject for interesting images. In these poems, night comes alive in some powerful ways:

A black-cloaked man
surrounds me:
darkness.

—MARY, AGE 10

Night, a black cat
creeping up on you
with the moon
reflecting
his eyes.

—KELLY, AGE 11

Night . . . a
giant
eating
the sun!

—MARY, AGE 10

Micronesian student names the wind *King* in this poem.

WIND, KING OF NATURE
You!!! Who are you?!
Where are you from, You—?
As I gaze at the grass on the hillside
I see you're at work, at your everlasting job.
You send green waves upward the mountain,
One after the other;

You make trees handsome and beautiful,
Like young men and women
With their hair tossed backward.

You make the beautiful blue ocean
Even more beautiful.
You create surfs and break them again,
Causing white parts in the vast ocean of blue,
Creating a terrific scene of blue and white.

Up in the sky,
You rule over the ocean of clouds.
You send them over the world with your order
Of where and when to spray
Your plantation of green.

Ah, you!
You crawl over me!
You're so gentle and caressing.

Where do you come from,
O King of Nature?!

—MARIA, HIGH SCHOOL

Kris talks to the sun in this next poem:

Stars fade away in the day lamps.
Birds eat at the darkness
Jump up, Sun. It is your
    moment!
Light the world with
yellow candle flame.

—KRIS, AGE 11

In this poem, a cinquain, we see the sun in a new role:

THE SUN AS BAND LEADER
Rising,
When you direct,
Clish-clang goes the cymbals!
You always get a headache
but you don't mind—
Good-day!

—TINA, AGE 12

Judy gives us a breeze that can whistle and skate. Can you see this breezy whistler?

The whistling breeze
Skated across the ocean
Splashing long, whispering sprays
Upon the shiny pebbles . . .

—JUDY O., HIGH SCHOOL

In her descriptive piece, Anne wants us to see not only a quick glimpse of a real deer but the breeze, too, as a running deer.

Everything is motionless. The sounds of the forest drift away into the stillness. Suddenly, a deer bounds across the path and fades off into the never-ending woods. A cool, misty breeze blows by, as if it were being chased by hunters. The forest is then left with silence as a bird sings softly every now and then.

—ANNE L., AGE 11

Jennifer tries to understand rain talk in her poem:

RAIN DROPS
Who's dripping at my window?
What are you trying to say?
You're talking too fast.
Slow down . . .

—JENNIFER, AGE 13

Tina writes:

Night,
in her black and white dress.
She only sees dark colors . . .

—TINA, AGE 10

Have you ever imagined winter as an icy power? Troy has:

WINTER
Who is the person
that shapes
the world into a
pane of glass—
makes a shiver
run down each
back?

Why does he
sting your
finger
and blind
each
house?

—TROY, AGE 11

A unique way of looking at spring occurred to Sally when she studied the list of spring words on our chalkboard. The usual ideas were there, including *birds, nesting, rebirth, eggs, warmth:*

Spring,
imprisoned
by winter's crystallized egg,
pecks her way out
to a season
of love.

—SALLY A., AGE 13

Sally took the images of rebirth and eggs and fashioned a word picture for us that shows winter as a crystal egg, with spring, an energetic fledgling, pecking and chipping its way out of the confines of the cold season.

You can see from the poems and images written here by children from fifth through twelfth grade that just about any inanimate thing can be made to seem alive, with either human or animal characteristics.

A group of children did just that, animating numerals from one to ten after thinking hard about their shapes and possible personalities. I asked them questions like these to help us see the number creatures: How does the number stand? Or is it sitting down? What other things are shaped like this particular number? Does it remind you of a person? an animal? a bird? Here are the results of this new way to see a group of very familiar shapes:

1 is proud
because he just got
new cowboy boots
and a jacket
with stars on it,
1 is!

—JANE, AGE 8

2 is a jockey
that bounces on a horse
towards the end
of the track,
fighting to be first.

—PATTIE, AGE 10

3 is like hips,
knees, eyes . . .
sitting around the fire
roasting marshmallows on the fire . . . Seagull.

—TOM G., AGE 10

4 is someone
trying to relax in the sun,
making a 4
with their legs
and lounging.

—PATTIE, AGE 10

5,
nifty, nosey neighbors—
half-circle, other square—
running sleepwalker,
upside-down 2.

—SUE, AGE 12

6 is a flower bud
6 is a rocking-chair
6 is a person curling up
6 is!

—CAROLINE L., AGE 10

7—
upside-down L,
ballerina's legs,
television antennas and angles.

—SUE, AGE 12

8—
Someone wearing glasses,
a small scribble design.
8 is a snowman,
bright, proud, happy.

—CAROLINE, AGE 10

9
is an upside-down 6.
He is a balloon
standing on a stick with one foot
9 is!

—JANE, AGE 8

10 is
an egg cracker
floating in the air
with a parachute on its back.
Ten was!

—TOM G., AGE 10

There are many ways to look at anything, as we have repeatedly seen. Two children look at Time. One sees it as a clock rushing us on; one sees it quite differently.

TIME
Who's creeping around the clock so rapidly? Where are
you going? Who are you? Round and round again. Every
move you make screaming and scolding, "Rush! Rush!
Hurry!" STOP!

—JENNIFER, AGE 13

For Jennifer, Time is a nagging nuisance, making us tired, pushing us to do things faster and faster. Is this the way Time appears to you? When do you get this pressed feeling about Time?

In this next description we see a different picture of Time:

MR. TIME
Why,
Mr. Time,
do you creep around
like a man walking
along,
Walking
so very slowly
down the lane?

—JOSEPH, AGE 13

Throughout this book we have discussed animation. In various chapters I have suggested that you look at a given thing—rain, wind, summer, the sea—as though it were a man, a woman, an animal. But in this chapter, I hope you have seen the broader range of possibilities for creating some surprising and satisfying images from some of the ordinary things we see every day.

In the middle of the day
I see dark shadows. I see
my arm rassing and it is
beack. And I am
juming up and down
shouting yes! yes! I say!

Our Inner Spaces: Moods and Emotions

We have seen that poetry can be the expression of a personal response to any kind of experience. We have still to explore poetry writing as a response to our own inner selves. Feelings that are not usually shared daily with other people are often the subject and theme for poets.

In this chapter, you will find mostly examples by young people of fourteen and older and fewer by young children. In some third grade groups, I did ask for expressions of feelings. But the results were generally ordinary and rather bland, with the exception of one or two examples included here. I think this sort of self-searching can best be accomplished by ninth graders, although you may want to try it with seventh or eighth graders. You can certainly experiment with it in the upper elementary grades, too, perhaps with quite good results.

But, it has been my experience that older children do want to write about emotions and feeling moods. Uppermost in the teenagers' world are their emotions and growing self-awareness—their self-consciousness. Expression of these sometimes overpowering feelings will flow steadily upon the page once you provide the impetus.

The poems here deal with joy, fear, loneliness, old age, waiting, life, and death. There are none about love, although this is the age-old subject for poets. And I have no examples of poems about hate, either, although this, too, could bring out some interesting writing if you'd explore its possibilities together with your children. The last section of the chapter explores ways poets can express many moods, emotions, and feelings through the use of color.

Let's see how many ways there are to think about joy. Are there some words that seem more joyful than others? What are they? Are there some special sounds you associate with feelings of happiness? Do you associate some colors with joy? What are some joyful ways to move? What is the taste of joy?

Listen to third graders as they tell of joy. In the first poem, Helen has used *swinging* and *dancing* to show her feelings:

Swinging along
on the nice breeze,
over the hill

and over the leaves
and dancing
on the big, bright, seas.

—HELEN, AGE 8

Crystall, another third grader, writes:

Joy makes people happy
and it makes people
dance in the street.

—CRYSTALL, AGE 8

In the next poem, we can see, taste, and feel one child's ideas of joy:

JOY
The colors of joy
are
Red, Purple, Pink.
The taste of joy
is
Turkey, chicken, and ham.
And the feel of joy
is
Fur, soap, and blankets.

—LORI, AGE 8

I've not, however, encouraged the kind of facile listing that abounds these days in the "unfinished sentence" (Happiness is . . . , etc.) sort of exercise. The serious searching out of the right word, the strongest, clearest image, tends to be bypassed if you simply ask for lists. When facilitating creative writing, it's that word *creative* that is the most important one to focus upon.

In this unusual poem, another third grader makes a delightful comparison in the last line:

Lava is like water
running down a hill.
A light is like the sun
in the sky.
And a book is like a door
to joy.

—DAVID, AGE 9

Do gold and silver remind you of joyous happenings? Those colors turn up in both of the following poems. First, one by a third grade girl:

You can hear the band
and horns playing.
You can see the elephants
marching
with gold and silver blankets
over their backs.
See the soldiers playing drums!
And look at all the people
with gay and happy faces.

—DELAYNE, AGE 8

And next, a poem written by one of the Micronesian girls:

A sunny day,
with no gray clouds . . .
A sun shines
with its golden light,
without any meaning,

but bright,
like a heart shining,
swaying back and forth,
beating like a watch
on a wrist,
and leaking
with gold and silver.

—OSIAOL, AGE 17

Two poets, from opposite ends of the earth and of different ages, use the idea of floating, of flying, with joy. They describe the essence of joy as a singing bird:

. . . You are happy.
You feel like you are floating
like a bird
and singing . . .

—TIM, AGE 8

The earth becomes a pebble
and the sea
a water-drop.
All my past memories
and hopes
are painted gold.
My mind wanders
and my heart
is like a singing bird . . .
I feel my soul flying
through the sea
and my body sailing
through the air;
yet, the end is so quick

like an earthquake
and
when I get mad
I turn red
and I punch
and scratch

—AMY, AGE 9

Here are two Micronesian students' poetic expressions of the chore of waiting. They are giving us their feelings about the unending tedium, the frustrating, annoying, tiresome business of counting the minutes, hours, days . . . waiting:

Standing for a second
seems sitting for a minute;
leaning for an hour
means lying for a day
and waiting for months
seems expecting for years.

Now the time and space
seem eternal and unlimited:
the ending seems
still the beginning
of waiting.

Days and nights
I swim
against the coarse earth
toward the unapproaching rim
of Heaven—
the horizon.

—MASAHARU, AGE 20

leaving my heart
hungry
for the unreturning
joy.

—MASAHARU, AGE 19

Cynthia's mood is evident in this understated poem:

Violence and war
are a waste of time:
ours
    and
        theirs.

—CYNTHIA K., AGE 12

Anger is a strong emotion. Look at the individual strong words that make up this poem:

Like a tornado,
his hissing anger
pierces
the silence
and
    levels
        boulders
            into
                pebbles

—WENDY, AGE 10

Listen to Amy's anger:

I am
so mad, I feel

Read the poem again, aloud, and see how the rhythm expresses the writer's hypnotic, suspended state. Have you ever had the slow motion, frustrated feeling that you are swimming "against the coarse earth . . ."?

This next poem is a similar expression of waiting:

Waiting.
Hour after hours—
waiting.
Nothing will be done
but waiting,
as an extreme punishment.
Waiting for a person,
I will not walk away
to comfort
my tiredness of waiting.
For if I walk away,
the person might come
that I may not be there
waiting.
So I stay,
waiting,
and waiting.
Waiting is tiresome work.

—ULAI, AGE 17

Loneliness is familiar to most people, and it's an easy feeling for young people to imagine, even if they have not yet experienced it themselves. A high school student once said to me, "I just think of all the things and people I love and need and then imagine my world without them, and I know how loneliness would be."

In her poem, Kathleen imagines herself to be a small boy left to wait for someone, in the middle of a city, on a bench:

LITTLE BOY LONELY
I sit on my tiny bench,
alone in the world;
the people bustle by me
and there is no sympathy
or love
in their eyes.
The buildings,
tall and foreboding,
tower
over me
like cruel giants.
I am lonely
and forgotten.
The workmen
are getting out now.
Their cars speed by me—
Screeching
and growling,
like animals
in the jungle.
I am lonely
and forgotten.

—KATHLEEN, HIGH SCHOOL

Notice her imaginative personification of the giant buildings and
the jungle-animal cars. This is an excellent example of the way
writers animate inanimate objects in order to allow us to see
those objects as they appear to someone else.

Moving to a new place, a new home, can often be a wrenching
experience for a child. In the next poem, we see a little girl who
looks upon a white rose as a new friend in a strange new place,
only to lose even that small anchor and find herself totally alone.

The poem is by a Micronesian student from a tiny island, Nukuoro.

A LITTLE GIRL WITH HER SECOND NEW HOME

Her room had only one window
to the East
that she could look through,
and see a white rose.
It was blooming
every evening;
she could smell it
through the window.
As time swings by,
and things change,
She looks out
through the window,
seeing somebody taking away
the white rose,
and she is left alone
with nothing
but the voice
of her past memory.

—Iemima, age 19

Here is an expression of loneliness for someone who is far away. Nighttime makes the loneliness grow:

. . . Soulfulness
is in me
as I harmonize the spell
of your name
under the shadow of evening stars—

for they form some distance
between us,
and my soul
always bears evening shadow's
burden.

—OSIAOL, AGE 17

Since shadows are usually without substance or weight, the
phrase "bears evening shadow's burden" is a powerful one.

Older people often have to deal with loneliness. We have seen
several poems about old age in other chapters, particularly in
"People and More People," but here is a short, evocative poem
written in the voice of the old person:

99
. . . Wrinkled face
and shaking muscles
engraved my body
for eternity.
Walking along my narrow path
I am entering
my 100's.

—FABYAN, AGE 20

Look at all the old words: *wrinkled, shaking, engraved, eternity.*
Why might a high school student see an old person as "walking
along my narrow path"?

I think of the suitcase
I carried with my wrinkled
hand.
I think of the camel hump

on my back.
I think of my childhood
and
I think of my death.

—MIKE M., AGE 9

This next poem was written in a summer workshop. The teacher has kindly allowed me to use it here. I am not sure of Russell's exact age:

ME IN MY YOUNGER YEARS
A young man walked up to a roadside stand.
"Whacha sellin'?"
"Lemonade."
"How much?"
"Two cents a glass."
"Gimme a sample. Maybe I'll buy."
That was me in my younger years.
Now I have a weak heart and live
alone.

—RUSSELL, UPPER ELEMENTARY AGE

Think about ways to use fear as a subject for writing. What makes us afraid? Writers and tellers of ghost stories know. They tell of darkness, of running from a nameless horror, of beings from other planets, of other times. Nightmares are made of the wildest terrors our sleeping minds can show us. We fall. We peer over the edge of pits. We see snakes, wild animals; jaws await us, floors give way, we see ghoulish faces coming toward us.

Use a whole large sheet of paper or an entire chalkboard for lists of fearful images, themes, and expressions. What animals are most fearful? How do they move? What do they find? How do they grab? Look at these words. What do they suggest to you?

tear	slash	scrape	slime
sneer	twist	claw	ooze
saliva	crush	slink	murky
creep	squeeze	slither	howl
silently	coil	glare	blood

Keep going—there are lots more words that we can use for scaring ourselves! Two third graders wrote these poems about fear:

THE MARTIANS!
The Martians eat people!
They eat flesh of any kind.
Then they take a knife—
and then they give your bones
to the buzzards.

—RICHARD, AGE 9

A little girl was sitting in her
house and all of a sudden . . .
THE HOUSE CAVED IN!

—JOHN, AGE 9

Micronesian folk tales abound with ghosts, like the ones that are terrifying the man in this next piece:

He's like a child in the forest,
surrounded by thick trees,
looking all around with blind eyes,
nothing in sight.
Soon darkness comes.
The rotten branches break
one by one.

The ghosts scratch his back.
He cries for help
but no one is beside him.
Screaming like shouting,
Shouting like screaming—
But, hands with no bones,
he's helpless
like an ant.

—OSIAOL, AGE 17

Look at the effectiveness of the phrases "looking all around with blind eyes" and "hands with no bones." They give us the sense of the poor man's feelings of terror and of utter helplessness.

Nightmares make wonderfully frightening subjects for writing, but only if you and your students remember to use the most powerful, carefully chosen words for your descriptions.

I'm falling and hanging to a vine in a deep, dark hole at the very middle, so that my intestine almost gets out of my mouth. As I look down, I see an image of a snake with open, waiting mouth. When I look up, a panther is there, waiting.

What shall I do with a fear of death . . . to bekilled in a snake's mouth or a panther? Staying there, out of spirit, stumbling, I yell and yell—unconscious.

When I look again, panther is still there, but two white and black rats are taking turns to bite the vine. As my heart starts to beat faster and faster, it seems to me there isn't enough oxygen to breathe.

As the vine is cut, I fall like a whistling jet plane toward
the bottom, heading for death. As the fear covers me, I
yell and yell automatically, waking up with fear, trem-
bling. Nightmare.

—ULAI, AGE 17

That *was* a nightmare! Two things work to make this piece a real
and frightening experience. First, the writer has written in the
present tense. We are plunged into a nightmare in progress. Second, the writer uses powerful descriptive comparisons to tell us
what is happening in the nightmare: "so that my intestine almost
gets out of my mouth. . . . I fall like a whistling jet plane toward
the bottom . . ."

Let's look at a nightmare from northern Minnesota:

It vibrated, pounded,
      beated and throbbed.
I squatted, stooped,
      ducked and bobbed.
It howled, screamed,
      smirked and sneered.
I shrieked, sobbed,
      whined, and feared.
If they were near, I cried . . .
If they were here, I died.

—CAY, HIGH SCHOOL

Cay uses rhyme that works here to form a chant of fear. All of
those active chase and evasion verbs with their *-ed* endings mes-
merize the reader into the fear that the nightmare evokes.

The ghoulish creature in this next picture has all of the fear-
some attributes that people everywhere give to demons:

She wears her mask
of devil dead:
a long, crooked tongue,
gums made of gray jelly
and a single iron tooth.
Most of all,
she cries
with tears of blood.
In tomb
and dark cave
she always lives.

—SULIKAU, HIGH SCHOOL

Young poets exploring "life" sometimes try to tackle the whole immense theme at once. A creative writing teacher once said to high school students, "Please. Don't begin your poem with 'Life is . . .'" The two poems included here seem to have solved the "big bite" problem quite well. Each poet narrowed the topic.

SOMETIMES I FEEL LIKE CRYING

Sometimes, I feel like crying,
When I see a blind old man
guiding his white cane
in front of him.
But my friends would laugh.

Sometimes, I feel like crying,
When I hear a song
about war
or love.
But my friends would laugh.

Sometimes, I feel like crying,
When someone is unkind
to another.
But my friends would laugh.

I wonder if my friends
feel like crying
at these things too . . .
but I don't think so.

There must be
something
wrong with me.

—PAT, HIGH SCHOOL

Barb sees her journey through life as a trip through a Mardi Gras, an arcade complete with colored lights, whirling balloons, and a hall of mirrors:

LIVING
We are involved in an arcade,
And we twirl and twist
Through its bewildering palisades of gaiety,
Confused and amazed by its brightness, and—
We are a Mardi Gras of decoration
As we wend the passages of blurred
Brilliance.

We are elated by the swirling
Redyelloworangeyellowred,
As we spring from ball to ball,
Our eyes fogged with cheer.

And then it is midnight—
In a hall of arched and smiling mirrors,
Our masques are unveiled.
What an unbelievable genesis is exhibited!
We have been masqued with ignorance.

But it is too late—
The arcade's doors have slammed,
Barred behind us.
The Mardi Gras has ended.

—BARB, HIGH SCHOOL

Death is another "big bite" theme; unless one can pare it down
to size, writing about death can be ponderous, bulky, even boring
in spite of death's impact as a reality. A mind-stretching session,
with words upon the board, is helpful. It becomes possible, then,
to explore language for its cutting edge. And students will find it
easier to avoid huge generalities in favor of a specific, crystallized
moment or idea or image:

DEATH
Sad man lives today
people happy him—
    to no avail:
    death touched.
Flowers bloom his smile now—
    only until tomorrow.

—NANCY, HIGH SCHOOL

The anonymous poem below uses words and their placement
on the page for effect. Using wide spacings between some of the
words encourages the reader to pause slightly (try reading it
aloud), and then a word like *glassful-smudge* seems to rush out

at once; *s m a s h e d* has spaces between letters, and the word is
slowed down—like a slow-motion film of the act of smashing.

SANS VIE
the
     lamp
lipped
its
         light
over the
     glassful-smudge
til
i
  s m a s h e d
        it
with my
fist-
     ful
      of
     darkness . . .

               —ANONYMOUS

Living on relatively small and isolated islands, usually in ex-
tended family situations, caused the Micronesian students to
have a familiarity with death that young people in our own cul-
ture experience less often.

In his poem, Arthur captures the slowed action, the dulled responses, the weighted feeling one has when someone has died:

DEATH
Ding . . . ding . . . ding . . .
The bell rang slowly.
Each time the bell rang

it would last
for a long while.
The windless,
endless
horizon died out
and left
a tiny space
of the universe
to pass the dead sound
of the bell
to the alertless ears.

—ARTHUR, HIGH SCHOOL

Look at the words one at a time. They seem to have been chosen
for their stillness, their heaviness, even for the sound of their
slow-going vowels. Try to read this poem in a bright, quick manner. It will resist you. Its language forces you into a deliberate,
quiet, sad reading.

A poem that has compared grieving people with ship passen-
gers who have lost their captain ends with this moving image:

. . . as the earth
comes running over
the grave
and the dark night
falls
with no moon
nor star.

—IEMIMA, AGE 19

We associate darkness, absence of color, with the idea of
death:

The gray clouds
come toward me . . .
the sky
is now painted
black,
and the body
is in the unexpected
home—
and sleep is forever.

—OSIAOL, AGE 17

Use of Color

Moods and emotions can be expressed in endless ways. One more tool can be added to the list: color. Most of us have our own characteristic reactions to color. We choose to live with certain colors in our homes; we dress in our favorite color; we often associate a color with a state of mind, a mood, or certain kinds of objects or people.

Earlier, we noticed a poem about death that used gray and black to underscore its bleakness. Here is a poem called "Black." What is its tone?

BLACK
Black is the life in the smouldering fire,
a tarnished old spoon,
the tongue of a liar.

Black's flat or sharp if you play the piano,
notes on a staff for the shrill-voiced soprano.

Black are the buttons on high-buttoned boots,
the coal in the coal-bin
the wrinkles in suits.

Black is a pencil point,
letters in print.
White where I washed the floor,
Black where I d'int.

Black is the face of a young Angus calf,
A poorly told joke
and a sarcastic laugh.

A raven, a panther, an inky toucan,
the rifle's report,
and the heart of the man
that refuses to pardon the faults
of all others
but expects to be treated by all
as a brother,
are as black as Death on her midnight prowl,
a voice in the night,
a hoot of an owl.

—PETER, AGE 14

Have you ever imagined colors that you can hear, smell, taste?
Try it:

GRAY
a musty smell
a dusty haste
a muffled sound
an aftertaste.

—MARY, HIGH SCHOOL

Think about lavender. What do you see? Is it a heavy color? Light? Can you touch it? What fabrics, textures do you feel? Does it have a shape? shapes? How does it move?

LAVENDER

Lavender is a floating feeling;
Heavy and warm in a dream,
Gauzy and light on a cloud,
Rustling and free in the wind.

It is the song of a sparrow on a rainy day,
The empty silentude of an evening walk.
Lavender closes in when you're sad,
And rushes away in your happiness.

—MERI, HIGH SCHOOL

Lavender, violet, orchid, deepest purple. Think of these, and then read Carolyn's reactions:

PURPLE THOUGHTS

Torn by the breeze, violet streams through the air until it rests on the first lilacs. Their lavender scent lures the hummingbird and the little boy.

Waking violets are found in May baskets. Plums are found on the tree, and disappear when people walk by.

Purple is in the crayonpicture given to mother. And purple rings out its freedom song on liberty documents.

Tyrian purple rides to battle with the sovereign. And orchid dances, caught for a moment in the precious flower.

Then—purple velvet drapes my world.

—CAROLYN, HIGH SCHOOL

Eight-year-old Kevin saw mountains when he thought about purple:

> Purple mountains.
> The sun makes the mountains
> turn purple
> and the mountains blue.
> And purple moves slow
> on the mountains.
>
> —KEVIN, AGE 8

Green appears all around us, and your children can think of many things that feel green. Listen!

> GREEN
> A dark green windy night
> Goes through my mind—
>
> The thought of seaweed and
> Masks shuddering over the ground.
>
> The color green stays in my mind,
> Emeralds, inchworms, lizards.
>
> We walk through
> The leaves with long stems
> And think of the frogs
> Upon their lily pads.
> We find a snake hiding
> In the grass.
>
> —DIANNE L., AGE 11

GREEN
The color green is like heavy gowns,
It is like waves of a sea.
It is a parrot rustling in the wind.

It has the sound of an inchworm wiggling.
It is the color of the water in summer.

The color green is like seaweed,
And the weeds in a lake at night.

—ROXANE, AGE 11

Have any of us ever thought of geese in this way:

SUNSET
Orange geese
come out of the water
and holding hands
in a V shape
they fly away

—GABE, AGE 10

And we can *hear* the yellow in this poem:

Yellow buttercups
rattle
in the garden.
How does the rain
fall?

—JOEL SWANSON, AGE 9

Does gray come to the reader in Bob's words? Read this poem
aloud and hear the gray!

The old house
on the corner
speaks a language
of silence.
Withered old trees
surround the yard.

—Bob K., AGE 11

And in the next remarkable poem, this *un*remarkable color
stands in our minds—unforgettable!

Gray,
a shiver of color
standing alone,
with no one to hold it.
Gray,
a cold color,
frozen in time.
Gray,
color of old things
brushing
its lonely color
everywhere.

—Melissa, AGE 11

Think about warm colors. Think about yellow again. What is
yellow to you? What else? How does it taste? Has it a fragrance?
Emily Dickinson, in the poem that starts "Ample make this
bed . . . ," spoke of the sunrise as making a "yellow noise." Can
you imagine it?

Orange. Surely you can smell this citrus perfume, see its glow,
taste its tartness. What else is orange? We have already seen
those geese lit by the setting sun. Is orange an animal? a bird? an

insect? Try a poem exercise that places something vibrantly orange or red with something cool and misty, like blue or lavender.

Can you see blue? Is it a mood? The blues are sad songs about
lost loves. Is blue a sad color for you? Does the mention of blue
set a particular scene in motion for you? Perhaps you always
think of blue in connection with another color. Blue/green?
Blue/white? Blue/black? Blue/silver? What *is* blue?

> BLUE
> Blue is a twilight time
> when shadows
> are among us
> and the lazy people
> stop sun-bathing
> under
> the cloudy blue sky.
>
> —PATTIE, AGE 10

Do you agree?

Most people can tell you about color—especially their own favorites. When working together with children, try listing all the
likely and unlikely things a certain color suggests. List moods and
emotions; list birds, animals, forces of nature, fabrics, sounds,
tastes, fragrances, plants, jewels, insects, musical instruments. If
we jumble them all together, what will we find? A skyful of violets? A trumpetsound of lilies? Ruby raindrops? Feather-smoke
gray moods?

"Our Inner Spaces" we called this chapter. They are a
labyrinth to explore. If you help your young writers to find their
way inside themselves, your reward will certainly be as great as
theirs.

Let me travel
through the air,
into the sky.
Let me see
the laughing man in the moon
and the sparkle of the star tears.

Now Let's Write About...

It must be obvious, by now, that under your guidance, almost anything can serve to stimulate children to write, no matter how old they are, or what kinds of backgrounds they represent.

Whether you use materials from the past or from the present, endless possibilities exist.

In earlier chapters, we have talked about the use of mystery slips which are drawn from a box or jar and contain an idea or subject to write about. As a variation on this, try having two collections of slips on two different colors of paper. Slips in the first color will have singular or plural nouns written on them. Slips in the second color may have verb forms or adjectives—the more unusual the better, of course.

The following poems were all written in one session of about an hour. Slips of colored paper were placed in two big glass bowls. The slips were folded in half to make them more secret and special. As each child picked *one from each bowl*, there was much groaning and forehead smacking, since these combinations struck the children as impossibilities. So, we decided that each dissatisfied customer could exchange *one* slip for a different one of the same color. Some did. Others decided not to risk an even greater impossibility. And the writing began.

Our rule was that the two words *must* be used *together*. That is, no other word could come between them. It did not matter in what order the words were used.

These poems were the result of this motivating technique. The mystery slip words are in italics.

Windy
rooftops blowing.
Sky is thin.
Wicked clouds
run away
howling.

—Kathy McD., age 13

Cars rush by in all directions
Odd feelings come to me
When near the *foggy streets.*
Shadows lurk everywhere.

I draw nearer to my father,
Clutching his hand
furiously.

—WENDY H., AGE 11

Listen!
The wind's howling.
Look!
The grass is swaying.
See the *treetops' shimmering* leaves:
Autumn.

—EMILY M., AGE 10

Strawberry windows
with sun
shining in.
Super-fresh fruit
picked out of a garden.
The sun sets
over the farm.
It rains on many days
in the spring.
Strawberry windows.

—MARY M., AGE 9

Misty doorways
like boxes of fog
with a board cutting the cloud
in half.
When the board moves,
misty doorways
are open.

—EMILY M., AGE 10

Lemon daisies
and
strawberry grasses
blend
with the plum shadows
of trees
to make a fresh, flowery
field of sweetness.

     —MARY ANNE C., AGE 16

This particular idea starter proved to be one of the all-time favorites in classrooms. The students spent their extra time dipping into the bowls for the two slips of colored paper that gave them, it seems, such a good push into the world of imaginative writing. You can keep containers of words on hand at home. No one can resist the challenge—you'll see!

Look again at Emily's poem beginning, "Misty doorways." It is impossible to imagine that, *without those particular two slips of paper*, Emily would have come up with anything remotely resembling this word picture. Under what other circumstances would Emily have pictured those "doorways like boxes of fog"? Boxes of fog! Have you ever spoken or written or thought about boxes of fog? Neither had Emily, of course. But once she began to see those misty doorways, they became real for her. The shape of doorways, the texture of mist, and synonyms for the word *misty* all worked together to help her to expand her imaginative vision. Only then could she tell us of this vision and let us see the solid door as "a board cutting the cloud in half."

Another way to use the simple, subject matter starter slip is to suggest that the subject itself never be actually mentioned in the poem or in the title. The idea for the riddle poem came from a session in which we read May Swenson's marvelous books of poetry, *Poems to Solve* and *More Poems to Solve*.

With an absolutely bewitching use of words, May Swenson gives us familiar objects, animals, plants, woodland scenes, and tells all *by speaking about other things.* In her poems, the answer is rarely given. Sometimes she does help us by putting it in tiny print at the bottom of the page.

One group of children printed the answers to their riddle poems upside down in the bottom corner of their paper. Try not to look at the answers to the following poems until you have really tackled the poem.

1. Swiftly
   on bent wire legs
   he moves without a sound
   going down a thin ladder
   for food.

   —MARY M., AGE 9

2. Prowling.
   Fierce daisy faces,
   staring with topaz eyes
   paws moving in the leaves.
   Sneaking.

   —EMILY M., AGE 10

3. Growling at the moonlight,
   looking for a fight.
   Sharp points stab,
   rumbling sounds roam in the dark.

   —WENDY H., AGE 11

4. Creeping
   garden hose
   with plaid back.

A lightning-quick forked path
Searches the air.

—MARY ANNE, AGE 16

5. Reaching
   twisted, crooked
   up toward the sky above.
   Arms pointing down to the dirt floor.
   Lovely.

—KATHY McD., AGE 13

6. Spikes hitting leaves—
   a wall of stalagtites—
   the noise is like tearing a sheet—
   enormous monster.

—CAROLINE L., AGE 10

7. Like scissors
   cut paper,
   it is pulled or it pulls.
   It makes a rumbling noise
   in the afternoon.

—PATTIE VAN D., AGE 10

8. Prison
   locking in teeth.
   Teeth wait for warden
   to come to take off the bars.

—SUE VAN D., AGE 12

1. spider 2. lions 3. thunder 4. snake 5. branches 6. rake 7. lawn-
mower 8. braces

Since the rule is that the subject can never be mentioned by name, you can see how each writer has been forced to see that subject in terms of something else. It is an exercise that is challenging to writer and reader alike.

Everyday occurrences can give us lively ideas for our writing. Shortly after the Mississippi River rampaged through the Midwest, I found myself in an Iowa river town. Turning the terrifying, inexorable force of the water into poetry was a way for the children to put its nightmare qualities on paper. It was a way to help them to put the experience into a new perspective. I was with these children for only a couple of hours, and some of them told me that they planned to write even more about the river at home because there was "so much more neat stuff to say . . ."

FLOOD STAGE
This year the current
went running through the town.
It wound through the marketplace
and climbed the
buildings. And made everything
dirty and muddy. It expanded
and braided around the houses.

                             —STUDENT, SIXTH GRADE

RIVERS
Have you seen the river knot?
Have you seen the river come alive?
Have you seen the brown river overflow
its banks? Have you seen
the river split and go over
the tops of houses?

                                  —JUSTINE, AGE 10

Another river is recalled in a different mood by Laura, a fifth grader. She wants us to see it as it:

> . . . flows down in rays of
> sunlight
> The river is a winding thread
> that sews the mountains
> together.

Notice how beautifully Laura uses the appropriate verb, *sews*, after she calls the river "a . . . thread." The ability to catch on to metaphor, and to keep it moving logically through the poem, is an exciting breakthrough for any writer. Children recognize its power and use it with obvious delight.

When I asked a group of fifth graders to define poetry, they responded with these imaginative lines:

> Words leak out from
> your fingers
> as you write.
> Your mind is color.
>
> —JENNY, AGE 10

> Shining feathers
> explode
> with words.
> They become
> a little poem.
> Poetry is wolves
> howling lies to the moon

The moon swallows the lie
Poetry
Is the brain, nerves
pushing the hand to write words
yelling lies.
Poetry is an eagle carrying
the windy lies to the sun.

—JON, AGE 10

One warm spring day, I asked a group of fifth grade children to think about the days of the week. Does each day have a personality of its own, we wondered? We decided to see what would happen if we chose Sunday to write about.

The collection of ideas on paper and on the chalkboard included words like steeple, funny paper, morning, sanctuary, stained glass, color, chorus, tulips, dandelions, daydream, ringing, quartet, pews, quiet, bricks, doors, windows, key, time. Quite a mixture, I'm sure you'll agree! The resulting poems certainly do describe the essence of Sunday.

A burst
of musical tulips sing in
the garden. I read the funny papers.
I hear bells and stained glass music.
It's golden to hear such a thing!

—TAMMIE, AGE 10

I lean against sun
    shattering on splinters of glass.
I taste the funnypaper
    in the sanctuary of morning.

I hear quiet time daydreaming
    through a chorus of cracked doors.
I value rose-stained, fluted
    chimes on Sunday.

—JIM, AGE 10

When the world cracked open,
Man played notes of color,
mountains grew high, rivers grew
deep, and a chorus of roses
sang like gold!

—BOB, AGE 10

The trees sleep late.
The peoples's wall of sleep is breaking.
Out in the open, bells ring out.
The chorus pours out with song.

—LORI, AGE 10

Elsewhere in this book, we have tried to use words to evoke a variety of sounds that have to come entirely from our imaginations. Stars sing. Trees scratch at a locked door to get our attention. Buttercups rattle.

Can the poet write about the absence of sound? Some nine- and ten-year-olds were asked to think about quiet scenes and quiet words. Ask your children to try closing their eyes for a few minutes before writing, and see how still the room becomes. Just *thinking* about silence has a hushing effect on us!

Ask the youngsters to list things that are the equivalent of "no sound," and see what happens. These poems ask us to read them almost in a whisper. We would not want to shout out the words of any of these poems!

SILENCE
Quiet
dreams of white moths
float in my mind
calm as time. Stars drop through
darkening skies
singing.

—FOURTH GRADE CLASS

Blooming flowers, shadows in
slanted alleys.
Butterflies fly to the sun
The wind blows the fallen
leaves over the wall.
Spiders creep slowly
in the fog, and a rabbit dreams
silver dreams in his hole.

—CHERYL, AGE 9

Can you imagine anything quieter than Jodie's simple, one-sentence image?

Watching
just one giraffe,
asleep with nothing on
its mind.

—JODIE, AGE 11

The five-years-olds in this kindergarten told me all the things they could think of that make no noise at all. This list is what they wanted me to take home. (Try reading it aloud!)

As quiet as . . .
a tree
snowflakes
a balloon
a pumpkin smiling
a flower growing
a whisper
lighting a candle
milk
setting a clock
petting a dog
falling asleep

—KINDERGARTEN CHILDREN

Eric sees silence as a person:

Silence has a next door neighbor
named noise.
His door is made by Time.
His house is made of rainbows.

—ERIC, AGE 7

Anyone who has stood outside on a freezing cold night, when
the temperature has slid far below zero, will identify with the
child who wrote the following poem:

In the last light of the winter evening,
the world is soundless.
The only noise is the stars twinkling
and the moon
lullabying the sun to sleep.
Soft snowflakes beat on the windowpane.
I am the only person in the world.

—ALISON, AGE 9

Many fine videos exist today, with more becoming available even as you read this! You can choose among videos that focus on nature, science, art, archaeology, history, biography. In fact, there seems to be no end to the possibilities for motivating children to write from a fresh point of view through the use of movies.

Still photographs can also be highly motivating. Most magazines today include a wealth of good photographs of people, animals, buildings, scenes from all over the world. Each one can be a spark-setter to the young writer's imagination.

Think about the kinds of questions that can be asked about each picture. What is the time of day? The weather? The mood of nature? The mood of the people or animals? Who is the picture about? What does it say to us? Can you become a part of the picture and tell about your own feelings? Answers to questions like these will start the writers on their way.

Use reproductions of paintings, too. Or take a trip to a local gallery and write ideas there on the spot, polishing them together later. (You will remember that this technique was also suggested in "People and More People.")

Let your children choose a picture to write about. Then, insist that the child use short lines, rich imagery, and inventive language to give life to the picture. Your goal for each young poet is, always, lively writing—original writing that doesn't sound like anything any other person would think of. Don't settle for anything else. Your children can be encouraged to stretch their minds and to play with words for the pure joy of it!

These sixth graders were given drawings by the artist, M. C. Escher, whose bizarre combinations of animals, birds, shadows, and skewed perspective make it impossible to write a boring description. I asked them to write from a first-person viewpoint, as though they were inside the strange situation Escher has drawn.

NO WAY OUT
I walk into a dream
Dark clouds overcome me
I squint into the shadows
Gargoyles whisper in sandy hills
Silent stars twist among the moons
There I stand staring into a dark passage
Trying to find a way out.

—SANDY, AGE 11

FROM A DRAWING BY ESCHER
In a ball of shining silver
I see me myself
all alone
in an empty room—
only my shadow
to keep me company.
I look into the silver ball
and see a man I've seen before
—a hand holding me up
with its fingertips.
Now I recognize the hand.
   It's mine!
I'm staring into my own face
and I see my own life leave me behind.

—ANGIE, AGE 11

Bob was impressed by two of Escher's drawings:

I look through my dream.
Crickets crawl on me.
Their skin is cold and brittle.

It feels like ice.
I fall asleep in the dark.
Will I ever come back to my world?

—BOB, AGE 11

My apartment bulges out
like a huge balloon.
But it's not like a balloon,
though it is rough and bumpy.
On the balcony is a
lonely tree,
its leaves like little hands.

—BOB, AGE 11

I've found that the drawings of M. C. Escher are surefire motivators for upper elementary children. This is the age when off-the-wall ideas are appealing, because there is such freedom to let the imagination soar. The poems included here certainly demonstrate this!

Here are some paintings that I have found useful in grades three and up: Pieter Bruegel the Elder, *Winter: Hunters in the Snow;* Georges de la Tour, *The Fortune Teller;* Karl Hofer, *Three Masks;* Winslow Homer, *Gulf Stream;* Paul Klee, *Tomcat;* Franz Marc, *Blue Horses;* Reginald Marsh, *The Merry-go-round;* Pablo Picasso, *The Ironer;* Georges Rouault, *Sad Clown;* J.M.W. Turner, *Snowstorm;* Vincent Van Gogh, *Church at Anvers, Starry Night, Potato Eaters;* Grant Wood, *American Gothic;* Andrew Wyeth, *Chambered Nautilus, Christina's World.*

The list of exciting paintings is inexhaustible of course. These are merely suggestions, to start you and the children on another exciting journey into the world of words.

Some Random Suggestions for Parents and Teachers

Peer through a magnifying glass at familiar objects and describe them in new ways.

See pond water through a microscope.

Using a microscope (or a microprojector) look at pollen, cells, insect legs, leaf structure, grains of various chemicals.

Using mirrors, see the mirror-image world Alice saw. Step into it and write!

Explore a variety of objects with the children. Each object should have a definite odor or fragrance. Describe each.

Take a flower apart and describe each part in new and imaginative terms. See comparisons you never thought of before.

Watch someone blow up a balloon. Describe it at every stage as it is filling with air. (Perhaps the *opposite* is occurring in the blower?)

Look at the sidewalk or street with a magnifying glass. Describe what is revealed: insects? particles of stone, glass, tar? Compare the cracks with something else.

Pick out a stranger and try to *see into* that person's real self. Look for clues. What do hands tell you? Eyes? Shoes?

Overhear a conversation between strangers. Write one sentence of it as part of a piece of poetry. What else can you add? What conclusions can you draw from what you overheard?

Try using sound as a motivator. Recordings of music, voices, pure sound—all can be valuable to the writer. Sound tapes and CDs of all kinds are available. Children can make their own tapes, too, and offer them as fodder for other children's creative efforts.

Find recordings of electronic music and try these. The sound is so unfamiliar that the listener must use the mind and *see* the sounds.

Invite players of various instruments to play a simple melody, or even a scale. It is a challenge to a writer to find words to depict the sounds made by, for instance, a flute, and to find words to describe the same scale as played by a bassoon, a trumpet, or a harp. Listen to jazz. Classical guitar. Play Debussy, Ravel, Prokofiev, Stravinsky, Chopin—try anything and everything!

That has been the theme of this book, has it not? I hope you have shaken off all doubts and fears and anxieties about what is the right thing to write about. Anything goes. You never know what simple suggestion from you will be the flint to strike a creative spark in a young mind that doesn't yet know it will soon be ablaze with undreamed-of imaginative powers.

I wish you well.

A Selected Bibliography of Books of Poetry for Children

Compiled by Jeffrey S. Copeland,
Professor of Children's Literature,
University of Northern Iowa

ARNOLD ADOLF
Street Music: City Poems (HarperCollins, 1994).
In for Winter, Out for Spring (Harcourt Brace Jovanovich, 1991).
Chocolate Dreams (Lothrop, 1989).
Sports Pages (J.B. Lippincott, 1986).
OUTside INside Poems (Lothrop, 1981).
Today We Are Brother and Sister (Lothrop, 1981).

TERRY ALLEN
The Whispering Wind: Poetry by Young American Indians, editor (Doubleday, 1972).

BROD BAGERT
Chicken Socks (Boyds Mills Press, 1994).
Let Me Be the Boss: Poems for Kids to Perform (Boyds Mills Press, 1992).
Alaska: Twenty Poems and a Journal (Juliahouse Publishing Company, 1988).

If Only I Could Fly: Poems for Kids to Read Out Loud (Juliahouse Publishing Company, 1984).

HARRY BEHN
Cricket Songs: Japanese Haiku, translator (Harcourt Brace Jovanovich, 1964).

JOHN BIERHORST
In the Trail of the Wind: American Indian Poems and Ritual Oration, editor (Farrar, Straus & Giroux, 1987).

ASHLEY BRYAN
Sing to the Sun (HarperCollins, 1992).
I Greet the Dawn: Poems by Paul Laurence Dunbar, editor (Atheneum, 1978).

NANCY WHITE CARLSTROM
Rosie's Giggle Wiggle Day and Other Story Poems (Philomel Books, 1996).
Who Says Boo? Halloween Poems for Young Children (Macmillan, 1995).
Midnight Dance of the Snowshoe Hare (Philomel Books, 1995).
What Would You Do If You Lived at the Zoo? (Little, Brown, 1994).
How Does the Wind Walk? (Macmillan, 1993).
What Does the Rain Play? (Macmillan, 1993).
Northern Lullaby (Philomel Books, 1992).
The Snow Speaks (Little, Brown, 1992).
Good-bye Geese (Philomel Books, 1991).

DEBORAH CHANDRA
Who Comes? (Sierra Club, forthcoming).
Miss Mabel's Table (Harcourt Brace Jovanovich, 1994).
Rich Lizard and Other Poems (Farrar, Straus and Giroux, 1993).
Balloons and Other Poems (Farrar, Straus and Giroux, 1990).

LUCILLE CLIFTON
Everett Anderson's Nine Month Long (Henry Holt and Company, 1978).
Everett Anderson's Year (Henry Holt and Company, 1974).

WILLIAM COLE
Poem Stew, editor (J. B. Lippincott, 1981).
The Poetry of Horses, editor (Scribners, 1979).

HILDA CONKLING
A Bird's Way of Singing: Poems Written Between the Ages of Four and Nine (Henry Holt and Company, forthcoming).

STEPHEN DUNNING, EDWARD LUEDERS, AND HUGH SMITH
Reflections on a Gift of Watermelon Pickle and Other Modern Verse, editors (Lothrop, Lee & Shepard, 1967).
Some Haystacks Don't Even Have Any Needle: And Other Complete Modern Poems, editors (Lothrop, Lee & Shepard, 1969).

BARBARA JUSTER ESBENSEN
The Night Rainbow: Images of the Northern Lights from Around the World (HarperCollins, forthcoming).
Around the World (Harper Collins, forthcoming).
Echoes for the Eye: Poems to Celebrate Patterns in Nature (HarperCollins, forthcoming).
Dance with Me (HarperCollins, 1995).
Who Shrank My Grandmother's House: Poems of Discovery (HarperCollins, 1992).
Words with Wrinkled Knees (Harper & Row, 1986).
Cold Stars and Fireflies (Harper & Row, 1984).
Swing Around the Sun (Lerner Publications, 1965).

AILEEN FISHER
Always Wondering: Some Favorite Poems of Aileen Fisher (HarperCollins, 1991).
When It Comes to Bugs (HarperCollins, 1986).
Rabbits, Rabbits (HarperCollins, 1983).

Out in the Dark and Daylight (HarperCollins, 1980).
My Cat Has Eyes of Sapphire Blue (Thomas Y. Crowell, 1973).

ROBERT FROST
You Come Too (Henry Holt and Company, 1959).

NIKKI GIOVANNI
Twenty-fifth Anniversary of Ego Tripping and Other Poems for Young Readers (Chicago Review Press, 1994).
My House: Poems (Morrow, 1972, revised edition, 1983).
Spin a Soft Black Song: Poems for Children (Hill & Wang, 1971).

MEL GLENN
Class Dismissed: High School Poems (Clarion Books, 1982).
Class Dismissed II: More High School Poems (Clarion Books, 1986).

ELOISE GREENFIELD
Night on Neighborhood Street (Dial Books, 1991).
Nathaniel Talking (Black Butterfly Children's Books, 1989).
Under the Sunday Tree (HarperCollins, 1988).
Daydreamers (Dial Books, 1981).

HAROLD G. HENDERSON
An Introduction to Haiku: An Anthology of Poems and Poets from Bashō to Shiki (Doubleday, 1958).

MARY ANN HOBERMAN
Fathers, Mothers, Sisters, Brothers: A Collection of Family Poems (Little, Brown, 1991).
Yellow Butter, Purple Jelly, Red Jam, Black Bread (Viking, 1981).
The Raucous Auk: A Menagerie of Poems (Viking, 1973).

FLORA M. HOOD
The Turquoise Horse: Prose and Poetry of the American Indian (Putnam, 1972).

LEE BENNETT HOPKINS

Ring Out Wild Bells: Poems for Holidays and Seasons (Harcourt Brace Jovanovich, 1992).

Through Our Eyes (Little, Brown, 1992).

Happy Birthday (Simon and Schuster, 1991).

On the Farm (Little, Brown, 1991).

Side by Side: Poems to Read Together (Simon and Schuster, 1988).

Still As a Star: Nighttime Poems (Little, Brown, 1989).

Rainbows Are Made: Poems by Carl Sandburg, editor (Harcourt Brace Jovanovich, 1982).

Morning, Noon, and Nighttime, Too (HarperCollins, 1980).

PATRICIA HUBBELL

A Grass Green Gallop (Atheneum, 1990).

The Tigers Brought Pink Lemonade (Atheneum, 1988).

LANGSTON HUGHES

Don't You Turn Back (Alfred A. Knopf, 1969).

PAUL JANECZKO

Stardust Hotel (Orchard Books, 1993).

Brickyard Summer (Orchard Books, 1989).

Going Over to Your Place: Poems for Each Other, editor, (Bradbury Press, 1987).

Strings: A Gathering of Family Poems, editor (Bradbury Press, 1984).

JUNE JORDAN AND TERRI BUSH

The Voice of the Children, editors (Holt, Rinehart and Winston, 1970).

STEPHEN M. JOSEPH

The Me Nobody Knows: Children's Voices from the Ghetto (Avon, 1972).

X. J. KENNEDY

Talking Like the Rain: A Read-to-Me Book of Poems, with Dorothy M. Kennedy (Little, Brown, 1992).

The Kite That Braved Old Orchard Beach: Year-Round Poems for Young People (McElderry/Macmillan, 1991).

The Forgetful Wishing Well: Poems for Young People (McElderry/Macmillan, 1985).

Knock At a Star: A Child's Introduction to Poetry, with Dorothy M. Kennedy (Little, Brown, 1985).

KARLA KUSKIN

Something Sleeping in the Hall (HarperCollins, 1985).

Dogs and Dragons, Trees and Dreams (Harper & Row, 1980).

Near the Window Tree: Poems and Notes (Harper & Row, 1975).

Any Me I Want to Be (Harper & Row, 1972).

NANCY LARRICK

I Heard a Scream in the Street: Poems by Young People in the City, editor (M. Evans and Company, 1970).

CONSTANCE LEVY

A Tree Place and Other Poems (Margaret McElderry/Macmillan, 1994).

I'm Going to Pet a Worm Today, and Other Poems (Margaret McElderry/Macmillan, 1991).

J. PATRICK LEWIS

Black Swan/White Crow (Atheneum, 1995).

The Fat-Cats at Sea (Alfred A. Knopf, 1994).

July Is a Mad Mosquito (Atheneum, 1994).

Earth Verses and Water Rhymes (Atheneum, 1991).

Two-Legged, Four-Legged, No-Legged Rhymes (Alfred A. Knopf, 1991).

RICHARD LEWIS

Miracles: Poems by Children of the English-Speaking World, editor (Simon and Schuster, 1966).

MYRA COHN LIVINGSTON
Remembering and Other Poems (Macmillan, 1989).
Halloween Poems, editor (Holiday House, 1989).
There Was a Place, and Other Poems (Macmillan, 1988).
Space Songs (Holiday House, 1986).
Worlds I Know, and Other Poems (Atheneum, 1985).

EVE MERRIAM
The Singing Green: New and Selected Poems for Young Readers
(Morrow Junior Books, 1992).

LILIAN MOORE
I'll Meet You at the Cucumbers (Macmillan, 1988).
Something New Begins (Atheneum, 1982).
Think of Shadows (Atheneum, 1980).

LILLIAN MORRISON
Slam Dunk: Poems About Basketball, editor (Hyperion Books for
Children, 1994).
At the Crack of the Bat: Baseball Poems, editor (Hyperion Books
for Children, 1992).
Whistling the Morning In: New Poems (Boyds Mills Press, 1992).
Rhythm Road: Poems to Move to, editor (Lothrop, Lee & Shepard,
1988).
The Break-Dance Kids: Poems of Sport, Motion, and Locomotion
(Lothrop, Lee & Shepard, 1985).
Overheard in a Bubble Chamber and Other Sciencepoems
(Lothrop, Lee & Shepard, 1981).
The Sidewalk Racer and Other Poems of Sports and Motion
(Lothrop, Lee & Shepard, 1977).

MARY O'NEILL
People I'd Like to Keep (Doubleday, 1964).

HELEN PLOTZ
Imagination's Other Place: Poems of Science and Mathematics
(Thomas Y. Crowell, 1957).

CYNTHIA RYLANT
Something Permanent (Harcourt Brace Jovanovich, 1994).
Soda Jerk (Orchard Books, 1990).
Waiting to Waltz: A Childhood (Macmillan, 1984).

CARL SANDBURG
Early Moon (Harcourt Brace Jovanovich, 1978).
Honey and Salt (Harcourt Brace Jovanovich, 1967).
Wind Song (Harcourt Brace Jovanovich, 1960).

MARILYN SINGER
The Morgans Dream (Henry Holt and Company, forthcoming).
Family Reunion (Macmillan, 1994).
Sky Words (Macmillan, 1994).
It's Hard to Read a Map with a Beagle on Your Lap (Henry Holt
    and Company, 1993).
In My Tent (Macmillan, 1992).
Turtle in July (Macmillan, 1989).

GARY SOTO
Neighborhood Odes (Harcourt Brace Jovanovich, 1992).
A Fire in My Hands (Scholastic, 1990).

MICHAEL SPOONER
A Moon in Your Lunch Box (Henry Holt and Company, 1993).

MAY SWENSON
The Complete Poems to Solve (Macmillan Child Group, 1994).

JUDITH THURMAN
Lost and Found (Atheneum, 1978).
Flashlight and Other Poems (Atheneum, 1976).
I Became Alone: Five Women Poets (Atheneum, 1975).
To See the World Afresh, editor, with Lilian Moore (Atheneum,
    1974).

H. VOLAKOVA
I Never Saw Another Butterfly, editor, (Pantheon, 1993).

VALERIE WORTH
All the Small Poems (Farrar, Straus and Giroux, 1987).

JANE YOLEN
Animal Fare (Harcourt Brace Jovanovich, 1994).
Water Music (Boyds Mills Press, 1994).
Raining Cats and Dogs (Harcourt Brace Jovanovich, 1993).
Weather Report (Boyds Mills Press, 1993).
Bird Watch (Philomel Books, 1990).

Poetry is a whispering shadow.
Words disappear
through the wind.
It's a mystery
waiting to be solved.

—DEBBIE, AGE 10

Poetry is
silver masks
taking time to listen.

—ROBYN, AGE 10

Poetry is the silken
door
made for
me.

—TINA, AGE 10

About the Author

Of all those writing today for children and young adults, it may be that Barbara Juster Esbensen creates the most striking, vivid, and refreshing—and at times downright unusual—images. Barbara is a well-known children's poet and poet-in-the-schools, and as part of her classroom visits, she often conducts poetry writing workshops with both children and teachers. She herself has been both a classroom teacher and an art teacher for grades K–12 and has taught creative writing to both young children and college education students. The 1994 recipient of the National Council of Teachers of English award for Excellence in Poetry for Children, she is the author of eighteen widely praised, diverse books for children, including seven collections of poetry. Barbara lives in Minneapolis with her husband and has six children and ten grandchildren.